Born Healers

Awakening, Nourishing & Training the Healer Within

Victoria Pendragon, D.D., O.I.M.

For permission, serialization, condensation, adaptions, or for our catalog of other publications, write to Ozark Mountain Publishing, Inc., P.O. box 754, Huntsville, AR 72740, ATTN: Permissions Department.

Library of Congress Cataloging-in-Publication Data

Pendragon, Victoria, 1946-

Born Healers, by Victoria Pendragon

Born Healers is a Do-It-Yourself guide to enhancing both your personal vibration and your ability to channel that vibration as healing energy to others. It also contains useful information for those who are just starting out on the path as hands-on-healers for working with the chakras and on how to structure a healing session.

1. Meditation 2. Healing 3. Metaphysical 4. Chakra

I. Pendragon, Victoria, 1946- II. Healing III. Meditation IV. Title

Library of Congress Catalog Card Number: 2016930188

ISBN: 9781940265377

Cover Art and Layout: www.noir33.com
Book set in: Lucida Fax, Papyrus, Nyala
Book Design: Tab Pillar

Published by:

PO Box 754, Huntsville, AR 72740
800-935-0045 or 479-738-2348; fax 479-738-2448

WWW.OZARKMT.COM

Printed in the United States of America

Contents

The Why of This Book

My job here (on this plane) is to empower people. This book is meant to be a guide, *not* an instruction manual. Please consider the words and advice in this book as a garden from which you can take that which appeals to you. Take from this book what feels right to you in the way that it feels right for you to do it. Go your own direction. Unfold into your own gifts. This information is here to assist you with your own transformation and development as much as it is here to help you help others.

Those of you who are going on to teach others may feel free to use this copyrighted book, in its entirety or in part, to pass information on to your students. If the information is amended in any way, however, I urge you to acknowledge that fact. While I am happy to take responsibility for my own words and information, I take no responsibility for anyone else's.

This is as it should be. Go forth and practice with integrity.

The day will come when, after harnessing space, the winds, the tides and gravitation, we shall harness for God the energies of love. And on that day, for the second time in the history of the world, we shall have discovered fire.

—Tielhard de Chardin

Foreword

In 1988, as the result of a mysterious allergic response to an herbal remedy that was supposed to whip my intestinal tract into shape so that I could—please Universe!—stop passing gas all the time, I ended up with a generally fatal, incurable disease that is known to most people by the name *scleroderma*. Its proper name, in my case—which was a very bad case, indeed—was the more technical name: *diffuse progressive systemic sclerosis*. Within mere months after taking the herbal remedy that was designed to eliminate candida from my system, my body began to turn to something far more like wood than flesh—inside and out—as it began transitioning from normal tissue to scar tissue. It was scleroderma—and my healing from it—that introduced me to the world of alternative healing.

Scleroderma was painful beyond description and it was frightening ... at first ... until I began to catch on to what was going on at another level, until I became aware that I was actually being offered an opportunity, a kind of a back way in to becoming the best person I could possibly be ... for that moment anyway, for as long as I might live. I lived the disease as if it were an adventure, following my gut responses to the opportunities that arose for me in the same way that a child might chase a butterfly. After about two and a half years I was declared completely free of disease and was on my way back to having a normal body again.

Fifteen years and a boatload of therapy later, long after my so-called miraculous healing had completed itself, functioning now as a hands-on healer myself, I was finally able to intellectually grasp enough of what had been going on in my body at a totally unconscious level to be able to codify it into a form that could/might be useful to other people who found themselves dealing with problems for which there seemed to be no solutions. After sharing the technique, which I called Sleep Magic, with my healing clients, using it myself for about eight years, and seeing wonderful results all around, I wrote a book about it which was published by Ozark Mountain Publishing under the title, *Sleep Magic: Surrender to Success.*

In the Bible the form of energy work that we all have available to us—the kind Jesus did—was called the laying on of hands. People have been doing it for centuries. You need neither initiations nor attunements to pass healing energy to another living being. We do, though, live in a cynical time, and in these days everybody wants to know what kind of credentials you have. But how do you get credentials for hands-on healing? Well, you can get those attunements that I just said that you didn't need. That's precisely why I got my first Reiki attunements, but you don't have to.

I had been told by a coworker with a headache that I had "The Gift," that I could make her headache go away. Despite the fact that I'd heard many times, from the healers who had worked with me while I was healing from scleroderma, that I did, indeed, have The Gift, I was dubious and I had no idea at all how to proceed with this woman and her insistence that I make her headache go away.

"You'll know what to do," she told me, and insisted on seeing me after work. And indeed, when I tried it out, it seemed that I did have the gift in question. Not only did her headache go away, I had felt things, curious sensations that I found difficult to identify, sensations I now know were energy moving. Both she and my husband insisted that this was something that I needed to make available to those who might need it, but I was mystified about how to put that out in the world. Would I just say, "Hey, I can help you with that headache, come on over to my house, I have The Gift?" How nuts would that sound? So I decided that, if I got some sort of official certification, then I could say, "Come on over to my house, I'm a level-one Reiki practitioner." So I got an attunement and that's just what I did.

I went on to get second-level and third-level attunements, eventually becoming a Reiki master because from what I could see it looked as if certification level mattered a great deal to people. And the certifications were fun, a chance to bliss out and receive some high-level energetic input; I liked them. I went on to perform them on my higher self and discovered that giving attunements was even better than getting them; it was a veritable spiritual high.

The attunements gave me a confidence in myself and in my abilities that I didn't have before them. So they helped. They opened my mind to the possibility that I could do what I'd only recently discovered that I *could* do. And attunements actually do *do* something. Attunements open up pathways of energy; they clear out blockages. In many ways an attunement is like a huge healing session on your whole Body-Mind-Soul-Spirit being ... but you can do healing work and be powerfully effective even without them and your skills and power, as you use them, will grow. Why? Because giving really is better than getting and when you heal others, when you use your energy to open and clear their energy, it happens to you too. We are here to heal each other in all kinds of ways.

Deciding upon having attunements is totally up to you. It seems to me that we are designed to heal with our energy, each and every one of us, on our own. My own energy grew with each passing year that I practiced hands-on work. I practiced for fifteen years. Why did I stop? Because I became a vehicle for the transmission of the technique I call Sleep Magic that empowers everyone to actually change the emotional cellular programming of their bodies, and it was time to put my energies behind getting that out into the world where it is much needed.

That work, Sleep Magic, is designed for cell-deep, soul-deep emotional healing, the kind that clears energetic balances and frees up life force energy, but it is a do-it-yourself technique and so can only work for you. If you want to be of service to others, hands-on healing is the way to go for it offers not only the healing that *you* bring but the very necessary caring physical contact that humanity thrives on.

The principles of healing that I pass on in this book are founded in the use of intuition, hence anyone desiring to make a more informed use of their inborn own gifts can use it.

Fundamentals

The Quadrinity of the Human Being: Spirit, Soul, Body, Mind

We are more than simply, as the song goes, spirits in the material world. We are complex, inter-dimensional embodiments, so before we learn a bit about how to best navigate this magnificent vehicle that we are through life, let's look under the hood.

The energetic component of spirit is the activating force of the body. When Spirit leaves, the body dies, not vice versa. And, just as the physical body has a passion to be alive, Spirit has a passion to experience that aliveness. Spirit has a passion for experiences of all sorts.

Spirit and body have a sort of a contract. You have no doubt heard it said that we pick our parents. In doing so, we pick our bodies too. It's logical when you think about it. The body you inhabit is integral to the nature and the passion and the desires of your spirit.

Your mind is generated by your body; specifically, it is generated by the brain. The mind is a calculator, an observer of details, and a recorder of incidents. Most people are all too well aware of their minds; the mind makes sure of that!

Your spirit is the essence of you. It is what makes you, *you*. Spirit, as I am using the term, is a metaphor for the infusion of whatever energy you think, feel, or believe is generating the Universe. Your spirit is part of that, as are all spirits. And all spirits are different. We are, taken as a whole species, like facets on an immense diamond, each of us reflecting the light in our own way.

Spirit is here for the party. And, at the spirit level of being, it's all a party. Because spirit is pure energy and energy just *is.* Energy, despite what you may have heard colloquially, is neither good nor bad. It is just that we, as humans tend to qualify everything. So we qualify energy as well. But as spirits, all we do is *experience* energy.

As humans, anger is a very unpleasant way to experience energy, and we tend to call it "bad." Spirit doesn't judge anger; Spirit eats it up. Anger is just one of the many sensations that Spirit is here to experience. Why? Because anger is just another way to experience energy, and Spirit is here *to* experience.

Some spirits are more adventuresome than others. Some spirits want to be on the fast track. They want to cram as much learning into one lifetime as they can. Those spirits will inevitably choose a life of high energy. It might be the high energy of an abusive childhood or the high energy of a serious drug addiction or the high energy of deep-sea diving or teaching in a high-risk school system. Whatever type of life experience it is that Spirit has picked, it has done so for its own reasons.

Other spirits are more easygoing. Their idea of embodied learning may take the form of everyday accidents and job-hunting issues. We are all spirits in this material world, and we are all different. And, bottom line, it is Spirit that runs the show. If you have spent your whole life feeling sorry for yourself because you've had such a hideous life, you might want to consider looking at it from another perspective, the perspective of what on earth could my spirit have been thinking? Spirits, of course, don't think, they simply are, but in asking yourself that question, you, as a being that *does* think, may get some answers that can allow you to view your life from an entirely different vantage point and that can be helpful because it has been scientifically proven that it is not our genetics alone that shape our lives, nor our environment per se that shapes our lives; it is, rather, our *perception* of our environment that shapes our lives. Perception dwells in the mind.

The idea that it is our perception rather than our genetics or our environment that shapes our lives is a very spiritual scientific conclusion, but Dr. Bruce Lipton lays it out point by point in his book, *The Biology of Belief.* It's a heavy book, complex in the science it is teaching, but the conclusion is as simple and elegant as any mathematical proof: what you think affects what happens to you. Thinking itself is heavily influenced by the unconscious cellular programming in your body so who you are at a cellular level affects what you think before that thinking has a chance to affect you.

Spirit is in charge. Your job and my job is to figure out, if we don't already know, what Spirit is up to. The sooner you can make peace with the passionate force that is the Spirit moving your life, the sooner you can open up to that particular flow in the stream of passion. When people speak of "coming to peace" with the life they have lived, it is the spirit level of their being with which they have come to peace. Once you have come to peace with the needs and desires of your spirit, you get to experience passion because Spirit *is* passion.

Spirit is that part of you that stays young, the part that says— no matter your age—"I may be fifty or sixty or seventy years old or whatever but inside I still feel as if I'm only eighteen" or, as in my case, four. Whatever age it is that you feel like, it's usually decades younger than you are. Each person has their own particular relationship with their life on earth.

Now the soul is another matter altogether. Sometimes people mistake the soul for the spirit and vice versa. I suppose the reasons for that are twofold. First of all, you can't see either of them, and second, very few people address the differences between the two. With the help of an extended metaphor, I will address those differences now.

Imagine the following scenario. It is a hot day, a very hot day, we are on a tropical island just outside an upscale hotel. A white limousine with dark-tinted windows has just pulled under the large porte cocher where any number of hotel employees, all in their uniforms, are waiting to attend to the passenger of the limousine. The driver exits his door and walks around to the passenger door on the opposite side. He opens the door. One beautifully shaped leg slides into view closely followed by another. The shoes are fabulous, with almost impossibly high heels but they are perfectly balanced, as is the handsome woman who emerges to stand on them.

The woman exits the car and makes her way through the door that is being held open for her. Back at the limo, the bellhop is busily piling luggage from the trunk to a shiny brass luggage carrier. There are so many suitcases and bags and hanging items that she is forced to carry some of the loose pieces draped over her arm. While the entitled passenger of the private car is signing in at the desk, the bellhop is struggling to backside bump her way through the service door tugging the overloaded luggage cart behind her while making very, very, very sure not to drop anything.

Just as the bellhop approaches the desk, the handsome, well-dressed woman executes a perfect quarter turn and heads down the marble hall to the elevator that will carry her to her room. The bellhop, attempting to appear as if this amazing juggling act she is pulling off is absolutely effortless, attempts to keep pace.

That elegant, entitled woman, energetically clicking her $700 heels against the marble floor, is Spirit. The bellhop, struggling to keep up, trying to hold it all together, is Soul.

The Spirit is the essence of who you are that exists as a part of all that is. Spirit is the part of you that *is* you as you in the grandest sense of your existence in every dimension in which you exist. Soul exists in the dimensions in which Spirit embodies as a human ... and it's the one carrying all the baggage!

The function of the soul is to carry the emotional information of all your embodied lifetimes. That's what it does. Somebody has to keep track. The soul is the living record of all that you are in every dimension in which you exist as an embodied creature. And that is why, if not properly thanked, Soul can get a little surly. It's a tough job carrying all that baggage around. Even for those of us whose spirits choose to experience life at a fairly easy vibrational pace, life is a tough job because, as humans, we experience loss. No matter how sweet a life we live, it will be touched at some points by loss. The human body dies. Animals die. We may lose the very elements of our own humanity that have made our life sweet. If we are healthy, functioning people, we do what we call *getting over it* ... eventually. Sometimes getting over it takes longer than other times. But Soul? Soul can't ever get over it. And the soul is keeping track of those losses for lifetime after lifetime after lifetime ad infinitum.

In distinct contrast to the spirit aspect of you, Soul is more apt to have you feeling as if you are Methusula. Being a soul is hard work.

So if we're smart, we do for the soul what that very elegant woman will do for the bellhop; we say thank you like we mean it and we tip well. Many years ago, when I'd been doing hands-on healing for about five years straight, pretty much without a break, I took a week-long class that was very much the equivalent of a modern-day mystery school experience. As part of our journey we experienced a guided meditation, led by our instructor, during which we were to take our Soul on vacation. My Soul and I had a wonderful time on a beautiful tropical island, palm trees swaying in a constant yet gentle breeze, waters the color of turquoise, just warm enough to be refreshingly inviting. We were paddling about in shallow waters when we got the call to come back.

I began to move toward shore when I heard, behind me, Soul hollering out, "B'bye." I stopped dead in the water.

"B'bye?" I queried.

"Yeah," it said happily. "See you in about sixteen years."

"*Sixteen years*?!?" I was stunned and more than a little concerned.

From somewhere outside my reverie I heard the facilitator impressing upon us the need to return to a state of normal consciousness. I looked at my soul; my soul looked back at me. Soul looked just about as happy as I felt perplexed. I didn't know what to do. I was supposed to go back. Soul waved as it smiled at me, clearly intent on staying right where it was, and I had pretty much no choice but to swim back to the so-called real world, alone.

Now I didn't come back soul-less, this was a metaphorical vacation after all, but I got the hint. I scheduled a series of soul-restorative treatments with an old friend who did color puncture, I cut back on my client load, and I took a long-overdue vacation. Finally, one day, months and months later, I was able to lure my soul back from its metaphorical rogue vacation.

If your soul is tired, you'll know it ... one way or the other. If you are what people have come to characterize as depressed or if you seem to be in a chronic bad mood, that's a sure sign that your soul is just plain worn out and it's one of the reasons why I am opposed to the more or less wholesale distribution of so-called antidepressants. These drugs have their place certainly; clinical depression often requires medical intervention of some sort. Some people need medication, but everybody doesn't! Some days it seems as if every other person I meet is taking some antidepressant or another. But we're supposed to feel sad sometimes ... there's information you need to know about in sadness; there's wisdom in grief, and both are signs that your soul needs attention. While drugs can trick the body into feeling perkier, they don't fool Soul even a little ... and they don't fix what's really wrong.

On the other hand, if you really know how to take care of yourself in a balanced, healthy way, chances are that your soul is perfectly content. And, just so you know, balanced and healthy does not necessarily mean that you meditate every day or do yoga. Meditation and yoga are both excellent tools for people who respond well to them but, like any tool, they can be misused and, like any tool, some people respond to them more than others do. If you do what you love, whatever that is, and are able to truly engage your consciousness in that activity while you are doing it—in other words, if you are passionate about your chosen activities—ice skating, roller skating, walking outside, gardening, whatever it is you love to do—that is enough for your soul. Treating the body well nourishes the soul, and a happy soul is essential to the experience of passion.

How many of us actually treat our bodies well? Certainly a lot of us think we do; a lot of us eat things we've been told are good for us and avoid the sorts of things that we've been cautioned against, but everybody—each body—is different. So as long as we're taking advice from an outside source we can't be sure—unless we've actually checked with our bodies—that whatever-it-is is good for us.

Shortly after I was diagnosed with scleroderma, the physician I was seeing prescribed a drug for me. He didn't ask me if I wanted a drug, he just told me that at the moment this was the only drug available and that it didn't cure the disease but had been known, on occasion, to slow the process down, as if dying even more slowly would be a desirable thing for me. I know that he meant well. I took his medicine home with me, read the accompanying patient information, put both bottle and instructions back in the box and returned them on my next visit.

I'd had a bad feeling when he handed it to me, and I had an even worse feeling when I read the seemingly endless small print on the crisp white paper that was folded over and over and over again, perhaps twenty times. Feeling is the language of the body and the body is always right. Period.

Sometime in the following year I was told about an experimental clinical study that was taking place in Philadelphia at the hospital of the University of Pennsylvania. The doctor who told me about it also offered to write me a letter of introduction to the physicians who were conducting the study. The rheumatologist in charge of the study offered to see me, at which time he asked me if I had been taking Depenacillamine, the medicine my doctor had prescribed. I told them no, that I hadn't. They were delighted because I was a good candidate for the study but had I been taking Depenacillamine I would not have been eligible for the experimental treatment. They needed pharmaceutical virgins ... and I was one. That treatment turned out to be a big part of my becoming entirely free and clear of the disease.

Listening to your body—to your gut, some people call it—is important. It is the most reliable source of good information about yourself that you have. Listening to your body requires awareness, and awareness requires a quiet mind.

Preparations: Discipline

We'll begin with the concept of discipline, a word that can call up unpleasant memories for some. But the sort of discipline I am talking about here is spiritual discipline and can only be born of your own desire to be a more effective and efficient facilitator of healing energy. Discipline here refers to your commitment to being the best that you can be so that you can offer your energy to others in its purest, most potent state.

I use the term *facilitator* of healing because that is what we become when we do this work. We most certainly are not the source of healing; that lies within the person on whom we may be working. Without their commitment to their own

7

healing, at all levels, we can be of scant value. We are, for all intents and purposes, nothing more than jumper cables.

The following information, exercises and rituals are all suggestions that you can use as tools to prepare yourself for becoming a more clear vessel of Light. The more clear you are, the more effective your transmission of energy will be. If you should find, or better yet, self-generate, tools of your own that accomplish the same results, then by all means use those tools! The critical factor is not what methods you choose but your commitment to those methods, your commitment to becoming everything that you came here to be.

Your own intuition will be the greatest tool you have. Everyone's relationship with All That Is is completely different from that of everyone else; honor this fact by using the gifts the Universe has given and will continue to give you.

Awareness

The body is periodically flooded by higher Siddhic states prior to full-blown enlightenment.

—Richard Rudd, *Gene Keys*

Only the human spirit can unlock the deepest secrets in your DNA.

—Richard Rudd, *Gene Keys*

I believe people who can control their attention, being totally relaxed in the moment and surrender to what is, can control how they perceive reality.

—Jeannette Brown on Ideapod

Our awareness is like a series of Russian nesting dolls. With each leap forward that we take we come to realize that we are housed within a wider framework than we had previously realized.

—Richard Rudd, *Gene Keys*

One of my favorite quotes comes from one of my favorite movies, *Joe vs. the Volcano.* It is uttered by the character named Patricia, a confident young woman who captains her own ship: "My father says that almost the whole world is asleep. Everybody you know. Everybody you see. Everybody you talk to. He says that only a few people are awake and they live in a state of constant total amazement."

This actually seems to be true, and it is entirely because people have not been taught to be aware, not just of their surroundings but of themselves. In fact, most people have been taught quite the opposite; they have been taught not to be aware. What they have been taught is to follow the rules— and just about every aspect of life has rules of some sort. They have been taught to be obedient ... first to their parents and then to others in authority, and "authority" of one sort or another can be found almost anywhere. Some people find it in magazine articles.

Most children begin to lose awareness as soon as they are mentally developed enough to be able to make some decisions on their own. That usually begins at the table, with food. Over five decades ago research scientists conducted experiments that "proved" (and I use that term *proved* judiciously, having read almost three decades ago that the outcomes of most experiments are determined by the intent of the experimenters) that infants, still in high chairs, would, over a certain period of time, if presented with what passes for a balanced diet, eat whatever they needed to remain healthy. They might not eat a little of everything at one sitting, the way we tend to, but over time they would, in fact, consume everything that was needed to provide their bodies with all the nutrients necessary to keep them alive and well.

Bodies are the ultimate source of wisdom and even an infant body is wise enough to recognize what it needs in what is presented to it. Most parents, however, were taught (by their parents) to kill that very basic instinct and kill it they do, demanding that their small child eats as they dictate, squashing the natural wisdom of the body before the child can even crawl.

Each one of us has our own very specific chemistry. Some of us need more protein; some of us need less; some of us are quite comfortable in temperatures of 45 degrees while others among us are turning blue at the same point. Most parents have never been taught to honor the responses of their children either to their diet or to temperature, both of which figure largely in life. As a result, our basic training in being alive, in being aware, is usually seriously undermined. Instead of learning to listen to the wisdom of our bodies, we were instructed to obey authority.

Add to that the rather common parental reprimand (because it *is* a reprimand and not a question), "What were you thinking?" and you have a perfect formula for distancing a child from his or her intuitive processes. When thinking—as opposed to *feeling*—is given top priority, then the path toward being a fully functioning embodied spirit is made just that much more difficult to locate, let alone travel to, and awareness stands little chance of survival.

Awareness vs. Consciousness

In the field of consciousness research, *consciousness* is very much about our ability, as humans, to be aware of ourselves. Other living things seem not to be aware of themselves ... but *seem* is the operative word in that statement because we don't know that for sure. As humans, we tend to be a bit arrogant about our very special selves. For all we know, every living thing—and everything, from plant life to rocks—*is* living—may be every bit as aware of itself as we are, albeit in some manner that we cannot comprehend.

In the field of medicine, the concept of consciousness is much more to the point: awake and aware? Conscious. Unawake and unaware? Unconscious. Members of the so-called New Age approach to life have taken the liberty of creating a definition of consciousness for humanity, referring to those with heightened awareness as *conscious* and to those with little sense of their place in the Universe as *unconscious*, another little piece of arrogance.

To be conscious, as a human, requires only a brain and a body. To be aware, though, requires something that the brain generates: a mind ... and the mind is a tricky thing.

The mind is like a big, big dog. If you've ever owned an actual big, big dog then you know that early training is essential. That little big dog has to know—ASAP—who's boss because if it doesn't, you are the one who will end up with a boss: and that boss will be the dog. That's what happens—at this point in our evolution as a species, anyway—to every one of us: our big dogs—our minds—are our bosses because we are, for all intents and purposes, trained to have it be so by very well-meaning people who raised us to "think, think, think."

"What were you thinking?"

"Were you thinking at all?"

"Think about it."

That's what we heard as children: emotionally charged reprimands strongly suggesting that our decision-making capabilities ought to be grounded in our minds, but as very young children our minds are not functioning as efficiently as they will later on. How much better this process would go if parents advised their children to pay attention to what their bodies were telling them, because even as infants our feelings are there, functioning every bit as much as they ever will, from the moment that we are born, and it is our bodies—with their built-in survival drive and their feelings—that know, at levels our mind will never have access to, what will be safe for us to do.

Those powerfully packed statements above—"What were you thinking?" "Were you thinking at all?" "Think about it."— directed at a small child are as potent as they are because they are fueled by emotion and because of that they are guaranteed to make it right into the child's cellular programming, where they lodge for the rest of forever unless that child later discovers how to change that programming at a physical level. As a result, thinking—not feeling—becomes the source of inner authority.

Why would we want to change that? Why would we want to relegate thinking to a lower status? Because the job of the mind is to calculate and to assess, functions that are valuable things when that's what the job calls for, but are not all that helpful when personal decisions are to be made and are virtually useless when it comes to establishing an empathic relationship with someone such as you might wish to do in the context of hands-on healing.

Relationships—which our lives are built on—are all about personal decision making. "Reading" facial expressions and body language can be taught when necessary, but the end result is never quite as easy as when the body and its feeling responses are at work. "Interpretation" is never as fluid as is a natural response to a situation or condition.

The entire body—its very DNA—is programmed in an ancestral way. Primal urges, such as the drive to survive that gives birth to the innate sense of "I gotta get out of here now," that arise in situations that may only subtly promise danger of some sort, are part of our genetic heritage and part of our programming. They are also the how and why of the reason that our body tends to know what is best for us since the body, like any animal, is inherently in tune with its surroundings.

The mind, however, can—and does—override this primal conversation with life. Most of us are taught to use the mind to override the body's own wisdom as we learn to become obedient to the instruction that as children we receive from authority: eat this, it's good for you; put on a coat, it's cold; don't wear colored socks, they draw energy from your body (Really! I once heard someone say that.). Most of us are not taught to respond to the quiet urgings of our bodies, and as a result, we may have become less aware of ourselves than we might otherwise have been.

Why Awareness Is Important

As a result of distancing us from the wisdom of our bodies, a tendency develops for us to rely on "information" gathered from outside sources. Most minds thrive on information and gobble up whatever they are given, judging the content as they go. Despite its inherent omnipotence, a mind can be trained, and a mind that has been well trained and knows its place can provide for you that most helpful of human gifts: self-discipline. It can actually help you to achieve the level of awareness that can assist your evolution as an embodied spirit, what some folks refer to as "raising your consciousness."

As human animals, our bodies crave the feeling of safety and of comfort; bodies have fairly simple needs. As human beings, we crave safety and comfort as well but in addition, because of our minds, because we are more complex, we also crave more complex things, things like intellectual stimulation, physical stimulation, and compatible company. Our minds—which are able to project possible outcomes—can provide us with distractions and goad impatience into becoming a motivating factor. It is our complex nature that detracts from the kind of full, present awareness that, say, a cat or a dog might have.

For many thousands of years, various sects and cultures have known the critical importance of being aware. The concept of being "in the now moment" is ancient and is the very same mindset that was cultivated—by necessity—in the primitive hunters of every culture. Primitive hunters learned to "become their prey," something that was accomplished via acute and unrelenting observation, by being fully present to their intended prey with every sense, not only to what any given animal was doing but also to what was going on in the environment around them. If it were not for those primal hunting cultures and their ability to function in the now, none of us would be here now.

Does such a skill matter in these more "modern" times? It does, albeit for different reasons for different people in different situations. It matters because being fully present is a mindset that allows a person to function at the highest level they can achieve. It matters to some of us who view life as a worldwide holistic evolutionary endeavor, because it allows us to see where and how we fit into the big picture and shows us how we can be of service to that evolution. It matters to some of us who create because it allows us to find our way to physicalize the dreams that are in our heads, to see how to get from where we are to where we need to be with efficiency. It matters to those of us who work with more abstract things—with numbers and equations and probabilities—to see links and clues we might otherwise miss. It matters to those of us who deal with people—and who among us doesn't?—to sense, in whatever way we sense best, things that the person with whom we are in communication may *not* be directly communicating to us. It matters to a healer because the ability to "get inside" another being energetically is invaluable; it literally guides your actions.

You can see that much of what I have just said has to do with seeing or feeling what is not immediately apparent. This faculty of expanded sensory perception is the natural outcome of being fully present, being fully aware. It is exceedingly useful; it allows you to become aware of information you would not otherwise have had, information that your internally generated calculator—your mind—can use to calculate whatever needs to be calculated. Then, in response to the fullness of the information that has been received and calculated, that is to say, in response to your awareness and intelligence, your body can then be relied upon to "inform" you of the best way for you to proceed. It is a process that is efficient, effective and, barring unforeseen circumstances (being fully aware does not automatically grant you psychic abilities), will always provide the right "answer" for you. In other words, being aware will take you where your spirit self would like for you to go more quickly and with greater ease.

Self-Awareness

Emotional maturity means that your awareness operates even during the most profound emotional states.

—Richard Rudd, *Gene Keys*

Minds are calculators and record keepers; they remember things (albeit not without some distortion), and they help us to figure things out ... as long as the things that need figuring out can be quantified. Because most of us are so thoroughly inculcated with the parental dictum of "think!" that we grow into adulthood thinking that thinking is enough, that thinking will solve all our problems, and it simply won't. In fact, the trickiest of human problems—which almost always have to do with discovering if someone, something, or some situation will suit us—can't be solved by the mind because all the mind knows are "the facts," and the facts aren't always everything.

Feelings matter; they matter a lot. And depending on how much the way you operate in the world is dependent on the structures that your ego process has set in place, you may not be as in touch with your feelings as would be helpful when making decisions that are critical to your long-term well-being.

The ego process is often known simply as ego; I prefer the term *ego process* because the ego is a process of the mind; it is not a thing all on its own. It is a process the mind develops over time to ensure that you do what you need to do, when you need to do it in order to survive. As a child this meant pleasing others. The ego process begins to develop in childhood, once the child begins to differentiate between itself and its mother. Early childhood thinking is very much focused, out of necessity, on survival. Once a person is in a position where they are no longer dependent on a parental figure for survival, the ego process translates what it knows to be able to function in school, the workplace, and the social world.

Unless a child has been taught to honor his or her feelings, the ego process will run the show until the (usually sadder but wiser) adult discovers a way out of the maze in which it has been trapped. And the reason the person is usually sadder but wiser is because if important life decisions have been made via the calculations of the ego process and the mind, then they aren't likely to work out all that well. What serves a four-year-old well is unlikely to fly at twenty-four.

Here's an example of the sort of situation I'm postulating: Becca, a forty-something woman in her second marriage, has just realized that she has married exactly the same type of verbally abusive man that she married the first time that she set out to find connubial bliss. Husband #1 had seemed delightful throughout the courtship save for one or two unpleasant incidents, which she wrote off due to the stress of the moments, but only months into the marriage he became more and more insulting and demeaning. Becca asked herself a lot of questions and got a lot of answers, some of which contained a certain level of truth and some of which were of dubious value. She tried various methods to diffuse his attacks, tried shielding herself, which is difficult to do when really bad energy is being directed straight through your aura and into your heart and power centers. After a couple of years, she applied for and received divorce papers.

Wisely, Becca spent a couple of years on her own, visited therapists of various sorts both in an attempt to heal and also in a quest for more information. After all, she reasoned, if I know what to look for, I'll know what to avoid. What Becca forgot was that (a) what she was "looking for" was hiding ... and hiding really well; (b) what she was looking for was not outside of her, but *inside* of her; and (c) what she was looking for was not a thing at all but a complex of feelings that had its roots in the emotional programming of the cells of her own body, a complex of feelings that had formed so very long ago that she had no way to know that they even existed, cellular programming that had developed during the first seven years of her life before her mother had divorced and fled from an abusive husband whom Becca never saw again. Her body had the information she needed, but her mind had little or no access to it.

Consequently, when she drew husband #2 into her auric field, assessing him with the best of her mental capacities, when she forgot that in the wooing stages of her previous relationship everything had been not just fine but really quite wonderful, when she made up her list and checked it twice and saw not even a hint that this new man was anything like the old one, she missed the most important assessment of all: how did her body feel about this man?

It hadn't felt good. But Becca, hyper-aware of everything that was happening on the surface of her new relationship, was unaware of what was going on beneath her own surface, unaware of the state of her body's response to this individual that had entered her life. He stroked her ego; he stimulated her sexually and was not overly demanding; he was open and honest about his flaws (the ones he was willing to admit to); he was kind and gentle, intelligent and clever, a good listener.

If you had asked Becca if she was aware of her feelings prior to marrying husband #2, she'd have told you that she was. She'd have told you that she was feeling a tad insecure but that she knew—because she had been very thorough in her assessment—that the insecurity stemmed from fear of the unknown. In fact, that can happen; many people fear the unknown. But for many others the seemingly baseless feeling of "fear of the unknown" isn't as baseless as it might be; it's the body, trying to alert anything it can get to, that what's going on just isn't right. It takes self-awareness to know the difference; it takes trusting the wisdom of the body.

The Role of the Mind

I have said that the mind is like a big dog; by that statement I do not mean to belittle either the mind's capability or large canines. I love big dogs; I've had—and all at one time—an English sheepdog, an Irish setter, a Siberian husky, and a Saint Bernard. Big dogs have their uses, but I know from personal experience that an untrained big dog is often more hazard than help. The same is true of the untrained mind.

How to Cultivate Awareness

Your mind, that aspect of you that can sometimes seem to be so distracting, can be your best friend when you train it to help you to cultivate your conscious awareness. The body responds well to patterned behavior, to ritual, and to habit; the brain, as a functioning part of that body, is no different. So once you train your mind (ego process) to help you, eventually it will begin to kick in all on its own. It may even reach a point where it helps you to see so clearly what you are about that you will begin to toe the line for yourself in much the same way that, as a child, you learned how to behave in a way that pleased your caretakers ... only now, you'll be setting guidelines that, ideally, make sense to you, your body, your soul, and your awesome spirit self.

Best of all, it's easy to remember and easy to do. It starts with simply asking yourself questions like:

How am I feeling (in an emotional sense)?

What am I seeing?

What am I hearing?

How does this feel (in a tactile sense)?

What do I taste?

What am I smelling?

These are simple questions, but they engage every aspect of your sensory system, which is the way in which you interact with the world around you. And you can ask all of them no matter what it is you are engaging with. You may think that you are simply seeing a tree, for instance, but it is highly unlikely that seeing is all that is going on for your body because all of its senses are working all of the time.

Let's use the tree as an example.

What am I feeling when I see the tree?

In an emotional way, that may be no more than a neutral or peaceful state, but it is a feeling state, nevertheless. But it may just be that there is something ineffable about the tree that triggers a more vibrant response, sadness or joy or confusion. That could happen easily because—never forget— your body remembers everything it has ever experienced, seen, heard, felt, tasted, touched, or smelled. To this day, the scent of myrrh takes me back to some place in childhood that I cannot identify and do not feel comfortable about. If I were troubled by that, all I'd have to do is visit a hypnotherapist and he or she could put me into a trance where I could go back and grab that memory and know what it's about. I don't feel the need to do that; I don't come across myrrh so often that it's a problem. Neither do you need absolutely to know the source of any feelings you may be having in response to something; you just need to be *aware* of them, and I actually find the response to myrrh a little intriguing; it's my own little mystery. One of the many benefits of becoming self-aware is a pleasant sense of objectivity that allows you to view yourself with a little distance, much as you might have if you were reading a book about someone.

That said, if it is a feeling that exposes itself to you often enough to constitute a theme, you may want to either visit a hypnotherapist or, alternately, use the Sleep Magic technique (detailed in *Sleep Magic: Surrender to Success* and outlined at the end of this book) to allow your body to simply let go of whatever is troublesome or, alternately, amplify it if it feels particularly good.

What am I seeing when I see the tree?

What *are* you seeing, really? Well, in the case of a tree, as with almost anything else, you are seeing a combination of things: outline, color, light and shade, shape, texture, relative size, shallowness or depth, pattern. There's no need to get all technical about it; you can simply notice the complexity of what you are observing and take that in.

One of the amazing things you see on a tree are the leaves, these little living receptors of light and moisture that dance in the breezes as they perform their incredible unseen feats, as buds and seeds form at different times of the year.

Often, if you look closely, you can see all kinds of insect life as well as birds, tree frogs, and tiny lizards both in and among the leaves as well as moving about the trunk of the tree, a trunk that may also be housing squirrels or chipmunks, or that may be dotted with holes where woodpeckers have feasted on the little insects that burrow beneath the furrowed bark. There may be lichens on the trees, lacey, green herbaceous doilies that feed on pure air.

What do I hear when I am looking at the tree?

Well, that will depend on where the tree is and, while it may seem to have nothing to do with you "looking at" a tree, it has everything to do with you being aware of looking at the tree; it is an integral part of the experience simply because it is happening. If, for instance, you are at the edge of a pond, observing a delicate, old weeping willow, your experience of that moment will very much be colored by what goes on around you. There might be the unrelenting sound of a jackhammer, or a couple having a heated argument, or a symphony orchestra playing Mozart. There might be what many call silence but what is, more accurately put, the combined sound of branches rustling in the wind, birds calling, the footfalls of a runner passing through, and other ambient but relatively tranquil sounds. An older tree may make creaking sounds in the breeze; insects, katydids, for example, might be singing their songs.

How does it (the tree) feel (tactile)?

The human body is designed to learn a lot through touch; pointy sharp things, for instance, make us back off. Things that appear smooth may not be, so sight alone sometimes does not give you all the information you need. Though it can be difficult to describe tactile sensations verbally—other than simple designations like smooth and rough—as we live in a society in which touch is not something that is given a priority. What we tend to do is to liken the touch of one thing to another: something might be described as being as *smooth as silk* (silken) or conversely, *like sandpaper*.

Perhaps somewhere there is a society in which people have as many words for surface textures as the Inuit have for snow (said to be 99), but if there is such a society, it probably does not speak English. Touch is an exquisitely sensual source of information and something that your body remembers very well as it is so intimately involved in the process.

If you cannot (or do not want to!) touch what you are becoming aware of, you might try imagining what the sensation would be like and, in the case of a tree, there are many different opportunities for varied touch: bark often varies from trunk to branch, and sometimes things like boles or scars from being cut lend variety, leaves (which feel tremendously different from their incipience to their decline), stems, buds, and even sometimes flowers, moss, or lichens.

What do I taste?

Taste, of course, is intimately related to smell; if you cannot smell something, it will have no taste for you, and if the texture of something should happen to feel inappropriate to the throat, the body will refuse to swallow whatever it is. (That's the body using its innate sense of "feeling" to protect itself!)

It might be difficult to taste a tree, but the smell of it would give you a pretty clear idea of how it might taste if that were possible. If you ever come across a sassafras tree and can scratch the bark even a little you will smell a strong spicy scent similar to the one that gives sarsaparilla, a sort of root beer, its flavor, you will be able to—virtually—taste it.

What am I smelling?

Trees have scents. You know that thing that everyone talks about, that "smell of nature," of being out in the woods? Much of that is the combined scent of the trees. Some trees, like the horse chestnut, have a smell you just can't miss; others are more subtle, but they all have scents. Those subtle smells are part of what attract the moths and other insects that feed off them and, often, raise their families in them.

Even if you think you can't smell anything, just breathe deeply ... your body will detect what you cannot.

You can try this exercise with anything ... or anyone ... well, maybe not anyone, but with certain people. Done with sufficient frequency—which will vary from person to person—this little ritual will train you to pay attention to— and thus become aware of—more than a mere cursory glance might yield. In paying attention to details, the mind is kept occupied but because its occupation is only with that which is pertinent to the task at hand, it is performing as a useful tool to enhance your awareness.

Awareness Exercises

The following exercises are suggestions for ways in which you can begin to train your mind to become more fully present in the Now Moment in order to enhance your general awareness. They are not the kind of exercises that you need to set aside time for; they make use of that which you are already doing. Use them as is or adjust and expand them to suit your needs and your nature.

The Ritual of Life

As you become more and more conscious of what you are experiencing you will soon realize the preciousness of your life and the life around you. Ritual has been developed over the centuries for more than the simple reason of tradition. Ritual, fully entered, throws you outside of yourself and into a sacred space. It connects you to the level of Universal Consciousness where this level of preciousness is constantly palpable.

The repetitiveness of a learned ritual allows your mind to expand on the theme with which the ritual is involved; you know the words and you know how to move, so the ritual becomes virtually automatic. It becomes, in many senses, hypnotic. Inside the trance you create for yourself while participating in a ritual, your mind, intent upon the subject in question, is also free to elaborate upon it at the same time. When you pay attention to your life, and you become used to paying attention to your life, the same thing happens. Life itself becomes the ritual and the ritual allows life to expand, to deepen in meaning.

Cycle-of-Life Breakfast

This could work for lunch or dinner as well but it is a particularly wonderful way to start off a day, allowing you to feel where you fit into things ... and where they fit into you.

Some people have difficulty envisioning things; they simply do not easily construct mental visual images. If you are of that type, then you must use your mind to construct verbal scenarios; as a general rule, most non-imagers have especially good verbal skills so be as detailed as you like, as flowery as you can be.

Our world is home to an endless variety of creatures but so are we. Our bodies are wonderful things, consisting of hundreds of different types of living things. Various systems within our bodies utilize bacteria to function properly. Microscopic creatures groom our skin and hair. Countless kinds of cells perform in a thousand different ways to keep various organs working properly.

The food we eat was once alive or in some cases, like certain cheeses and vegetables, is still alive. Its life energy is what gives us energy. Only the energy of living things can nourish other living things, and when we eat we satisfy not only ourselves but every living thing that makes us up. Our bodies transform other life energies so that all the life forms that make us up can live, thus keeping us alive.

Remember all this as you eat. Recognize that you are part of a cycle. If you are lucky enough to be able to eat outdoors, look around, see and feel that cycle in action as cats stalk birds that are hunting down bugs and worms, enjoy it! Enjoy your place in the food chain and give thanks for that! There was a time when we humans were a lot farther down the food chain than we are now!

Let the tasty, whole grains of breads and cereals carry you back to the fields where they grew. Let eggs take you back to the chicken. Thank the chicken. Especially thank the unborn embryo you are consuming. Realize what it is that you are doing when you consume various foods. Understand that another living thing has had to sacrifice its life that you might live. This is a critically important fact of life, and your respect for it matters because it helps to grow the energetic field of respect for life that surrounds our world. When we forget how it is that we are alive, and what we have to do to other life in order to live, we effectively disrespect all that other life, collectively lowering our vibration as a species.

Let fruits take you to the sunny days that ripened them and the groves where they grew. As you inhale the scent of berries, picture them in the fields. Picture, too, the people picking the fruit, packing it, the people who move it to the stores, the people in the stores who set it out. All of these aspects of getting your food to you matter. Enjoy your world at breakfast. What better way to start your day than connected to the earth that nourishes you and the people that support your being nourished!

If some of the food you eat has been manufactured, send love to the folks that must have been involved in that process and to the people whose idea it was to start that business so that other lives could be made simpler and easier. I have a diet that requires me to avoid certain foods that I miss from an emotional standpoint so I regularly find myself thanking the food scientists that came up with nondairy cheeses, gluten-free granola, sugar-free treats, and various similar delights.

(As an aside, years after I was recovered from scleroderma and had become a part of a thriving community of healers helping people in southern metropolitan New Jersey, I had the opportunity to meet and work with a wonderful ex-food scientist who had become a helping person himself and was, as it turned out, the man who invented faux cheese! I actually got right to the source!)

I usually promise my breakfast that I will use the fine energy it brings me to be the best me that I can be in order to properly honor the many lives that have been sacrificed that I may eat.

Taking a Shower

Cleansing is a necessary ritual, not just for social reasons but for health as well. Washing hands is universally recognized as one of the best ways to ensure against the transmission of germs. And water is one of nature's most profound and necessary gifts to us; without it, we die very quickly.

Realize, as you turn on the faucets, what is occurring: think about how the water is getting to you, the sources from which it came, the cycle of water from earth to sky and back again. You are about to step into that cycle. If you are fortunate enough to have fresh well water, your envisioning can involve the water literally pouring out of the earth and into your faucets.

As you enter the shower or tub, thank the water for cleansing you and begin to realize that cleansing by water is more than just a physical event. Water will absorb from your body any influences that you will allow it to absorb, and it will wash them away. It is the ultimate cleanser; therefore, you can bring to your mind any negative or unpleasant incidents that have occurred since your last shower and allow the water to take them from you, to wash them away.

This fact makes the tub bath a particularly interesting event as one finds one's self "steeping" in a diluted soup of the feeling emotions of the day including, of course, all the negativity. This is not as bad as it may seem. As anyone who has done a little personal work knows, you have to face your fears in order to let them go. A bath gives you that opportunity ... but I always feel as if a quick rinse-off in the shower at the end is a good idea.

Showering lightly *before* the bath, to wash the cares and the insults of the day away, might be an even better idea and also allows you to indulge in the pure sensual pleasure of allowing the water to flow over your body, a sensual pleasure that you would do well to cultivate because feeling good is what bodies are designed to do; it makes them happy, and when they are happy, it's a lot easier for you to be happy too! Our bodies are animal things, they love the sensual; we were designed for that and the shower is a great place to indulge, with gratitude, in this simple, primal pleasure.

The bath is also a place where you can, if you are so inclined, do some fairly deep meditation. When I had scleroderma and it was rapidly taking over my body, I was in a great deal of pain; the bath was the only place where the pain felt less and where I could enter a very nice trance state to do shamanic journeying. Logically, because of being surrounded by water, it's a great place to connect with time in utero as well.

In ancient African cultures, the hair was thought of as antennae to the Divine. When you think of it that way you can see why clean hair would be of utmost importance. Hair and skin are both quite porous—they have to be—so they take in energy just as easily as they do creams and oils. In bringing to mind the challenges of the day—especially any that are associated with negative feeling energies—you can imagine your skin and hair releasing, releasing, releasing whatever does not serve them or you.

As you shower off, you can enjoy the feel of the water as it falls on various parts of your body. Focus on how the water feels different on different areas of your body. Pay special attention to how it feels on various areas of your head. Few people realize how sensitive certain areas of the scalp can be. For some, orgasm may be possible but take care that you are well supported. A fall in the tub can ruin a good orgasm and a few other things as well!

Before you leave the tub or shower, thank the water again for all its help and for the pleasure it has brought you.

Eating Melons and Other Lusciously Juicy Fruits

Hands-on is best for this exercise so put the spoon away! That way you can get sensory input for you and your body from more than just one source.

But before you even think about eating, thank the fruit, the tree that bore it, the earth, the rain, and the sun for their efforts. Ponder the wonder they have all wrought in such an unconsciously collaborative effort. Thank, too, whatever human power it took to get you that melon: the people who planted, nurtured, harvested, transported, shipped, and sold it or brought it to you. Smell the cut or uncut fruit. Mangoes, peaches, and most melons, if they are ripe and ready, have a delicious scent that emanates right through their skins and signals their extreme availability and deliciousness. Imbibe that, allowing some measure of the deliciousness to come into your olfactory glands; it's some of the best perfume nature has to offer, and it is a sensual delight that penetrates your body more deeply than any flower because your body knows that this wonderful smell is connected to food and there are few things bodies like better than food. This is the smell of life and of living, and it is delicious in itself.

As you bite into the fruit and its juice flows, think of the rain from the sky that gave the fruit its luxurious wetness. Really enjoy the feeling of the wetness and the sweetness on your tongue and in your mouth. Imagine the rain turning into the fruit. In your mind's eye, see the fruit growing. Imagine yourself drinking sweet rain.

Oranges are notoriously juicy and have the added aspect of a skin that is saturated with scented oil that you can often see and smell as you are tearing away the skin. Tangerines are similarly endowed, although their skin is thinner as a rule. Still, the very act of having to enter the fruit, of penetrating its integrity, is a vivid reminder that this is a living thing and that it is about to give up its life to you for your nourishment.

I don't say this to make anyone feel guilty, but rather simply to remind us exactly how much respect we owe to the world of plants and animals. That we subsist, that we thrive on their lives, is a constant reminder that we must be the best that we can be for we have taken life in order that we do so. This is an awesome fact that few are educated to respect.

Delight that you cannot only live, but love the taste of living as well.

Eating Potatoes and Other Underground Vegetables

Potatoes and yams and beets and carrots may not be thrilling to the nose, but they do have subtle, earthy scents worth acquainting yourself with and some of their colors are fabulous! Tubers pack a nutritional wallop, as they absorb directly from the earth her minerals first hand. So thank the earth when you encounter these subterranean gifts for nourishing such a tasty treat. Imagine all the minerals of the earth entering the growing tuber knowing that all those minerals are about to be transferred to you, to help you stay strong and healthy.

Think, too, about the soft, warm, dark comfort of the earth that nourished these helpful plants whose life you are about to incorporate into your own. Appreciate the darkness of the earth that yielded these energy-bearing vegetables. Darkness can help in your growth, too; you only need to know what to pull out of it ... and how to prepare it for proper assimilation. Your own darkness provides the clues for what you may need to release or transmute to become the person you truly are, for the spirit that inhabits your body is pure light; it is from spirit that the essence of you comes and to it that it will return.

Only by embracing and accepting one's own darkness can healing begin and doing so can assist you to help others to do the same

Eating Nonfleshy Foods; or, Fruits and Vegetables Are People Too

I'm always amused that there are some vegetarians who pride themselves on not eating living things. It's a bit of an oversight. Broccoli is every bit as alive as we are, as a cow or a chicken is. If it weren't, it would be useless to us. We kill animals to be able to eat them, and we kill fruits and vegetables as well, usually when we eat them because, unlike a mammal or a bird or a fish, most fruits and vegetables are alive *when* we eat them; the closer to dead they get, the less nutritional value they possess.

Try this exercise first with one food at a time.

Make yourself aware of what you are about to do. Thank the earth for its gift to you; then thank the spirit of the food or the food itself for making its life a gift to you, for transferring its energy to you so that you may live.

As you chew your food allow your mind to consider the area from which the food came and the conditions that might have surrounded its growth. Allow yourself to be in that place.

Then allow yourself to be the thing itself; bring its consciousness to you.

Make this exercise brief and return to a normal state of consciousness fairly quickly. Altered states of consciousness are not generally helpful to the digestive process unless that is their focus.

Nursing a Child

Nursing a child is love. Nourishment will keep a child alive, but only love will allow the child to thrive.

Whether you are the nursing mother or you are watching a nursing mother, you are watching the understanding of love being transmitted from one human being to another. Consider this, for the ramifications of the relationship you are observing will last for the lifetimes of both beings involved. And this knowledge, this ability to love, forms the basis for all social behavior, since the most basic form of social behavior we indulge in is a relationship between two people. Larger relationships, such as families and societal groups, grow from that.

Remind yourself, too, that you are watching one of the most complete forms of human communication. The understanding of love is a profound concept. Yet it is passed from mother to child without a word.

Another more obvious exercise is to realize how literally the mother's life nourishes the child and to appreciate that within the never-ending cycle of life.

People Watching

When we watch people, people of any age, sex, or race, it is like watching some aspect of ourselves as we are, were, or will be (depending on your views about time).

When watching children, you can remember yourself at that age. Recall the confusion, the happiness, the frustration, the innocence, all the aspects of what it was like to be a child.

Being a child—a human being in training—is hard work. (It is especially difficult work if you suffered abuse as a child. For dealing with that, I strongly recommend the book, *Sleep Magic: Surrender to Success*.) When you see children, even if they are involved in joyful play, honor them briefly and send them some strength for you know the task of life that lies ahead of them.

Everything in a child's life is part of the foundation of later life. Realize the importance of this and honor your own childhood as well as the child that still lives within you. Relish the joys of the non-responsible behaviors of childhood and remember that you need to allow time for similarly playful behaviors during your adult life. The child within needs to be nourished; for that to happen, the adult needs to play.

Do not become nostalgic! Do not reminisce yourself into thinking that the best part of your life was childhood, that your best times are behind you. They are not! For while childhood is a time for few responsibilities it is also a time when you have little control over your own life. Your dreams may be your own but your schedule, your meals, and even your behavior is dictated to you by outside sources, loving though they may be. How much better not only to be able to decide for yourself what to do but to have the ability to do it whenever you like!

Remember that when you watch children and teenagers, let your heart go out to them to support them. Young children especially can feel love directed toward them. Your moments of compassion will help all of them in the long run.

Watching people in love is always a beautiful thing, and it is an ideal chance to nourish the love you feel both for those in your life and for love itself. Wish the lovers well either in your mind or right out loud if they seem open to comment. Positive reinforcement always feels good!

Watching people at work is another chance to feel good about human beings. Watching a person engaged in performing a task that they obviously enjoy doing can bring on thoughts of growth and prosperity. It's good for them, and it's good for you, too. We are material beings in a material world; prosperity is one of the material rewards of that world. Joy in work and prosperity go hand in hand. Wish it for them and for yourself as well.

If you should discover, in the wishing of it, that you do not experience joy in what you do for a living, consider changing your work. If you have constructed for yourself a lifestyle that requires a good deal of financing, requiring you, therefore, to have a job you do not care for, one of two things has to happen: either you need to rethink your lifestyle or you need to reframe the work that you do so that you can enjoy it more. A little sacrifice is often necessary for a greater good, but a great sacrifice for a lesser good does very little good in the end.

Sometimes, observing adults and their behavior, you will see behavior that startles, upsets, or disturbs you. It may be (check with yourself on this) that the behavior you are reacting to reminds you of something about yourself. Or it may be that it reminds you of behavior that was once directed against you. If so, use this as an opportunity to make a date with yourself later to clear up any unfinished emotional business that may be connected with it. It may be that the behavior is simply very negative, destructive, or even anti-life, in which case, consciously instruct your body to let go of whatever feelings may have been generated. All things are, inevitably, exactly as they should be so you can let go in good conscience simply knowing that this world is on its way to becoming better all the time; your letting go, your "allowing" that whatever happened, despite how wrong it may have seemed, was right in that moment, for those people, will actually help to fuel the world becoming a better place.

Realize that these behaviors probably grew from a series of unfortunate events in the lives of the people involved. If you cannot be empathetic, try to be sympathetic for the torture that the soul behind the behavior is going through. Your thoughts carry energy, and people behaving badly need all the help they can get. Judgment-free energetic support is the best you can do for anyone who seems in need of assistance in a situation where actual assistance would not be appropriate.

Behavior that is truly psychopathological is awesome, but if you come across it try not to become fascinated. Consciously surround yourself with golden light for protection; it is necessary. Often, people are told to surround themselves with white light for protection but white light is the light of the Divine, the light that draws to itself ... and you don't want to draw aberrant behavior to yourself. Gold, as in metallic gold, empowers your own power center and, with its metallic sheen, protects you from auric invasion. (This works well, by the way, in lots of less dramatic but still unpleasant situations.)

Leaving the area of negative behaviors is suggested not because of physical danger (although that may be an issue) but because of the subtle transmission of negative energy. Nobody needs any extra negative energy!

In the full complexity of reality, pure energy is neither "positive" nor "negative," neither "good" nor "bad"; it simply *is*. But in the world of duality that we inhabit, a world in which we are all affected by energy, by how we *feel* when we are so affected, we tend to label the things that make us feel uncomfortable as bad or negative, while we label the things that either do not disturb our status quo or that enhance it, as 'good,' or 'positive'. Once we reach a point where our awareness has become keenly developed, to a point where the ego process is under control and our ability to accept that everything is exactly as it should be, these distinctions become minimized and can disappear entirely.

Most human behavior is what we might tend to think of as ordinary. All human behavior is about being human, about being alive. Being alive is extraordinary! It is a thrill if you are open to it being so. Therefore, every aspect of it can be viewed not as ordinary, but as quite special indeed. If you think this isn't true, ask someone who has lost the use of even one part of their "normal" functioning how they feel when they watch someone who can function normally. Better yet, ask someone who has lost a function and later regained it! It's a thrill! I know!

So when you watch ordinary people doing ordinary things remember: there's nothing ordinary about it.

Inanimate Objects

Most so-called inanimate objects owe their existence to at least one animate being and often, more than one. Inanimate objects don't make themselves, don't design themselves. (I do not consider rocks and other geological forms inanimate. If you've studied crystals or vibration, you'll understand this.

If you haven't, I'd gently suggest that you do.) So what I am suggesting is that you become aware of the metals, the woods, the fabrics, the synthetics and plastics that are providing you with assistance throughout your day. A passing thought is enough, just enough to remind you that the lives and energies of other beings have gone into making your life more comfortable, more efficient, more attractive.

Think about the wood or the metal in the chairs that support you well, allowing your spine to stay strong. Think about the designers of the chairs, the manufacturers, the packers and shippers and the people in the store where they came from. Thinking—bringing your conscious attention to something— is thanking!

What you are doing with all of this expanded awareness is turning your life into a constant, living prayer of gratitude. It seamlessly melds your experience of life to your perpetual thanks, a thanks that carries your energy right to the source, raising vibration all around. This is how the world will heal, how our genes will move out of the primal energy of fear in which they are rooted and into the energy of cooperation and the celebration of life itself.

Advanced Seeing

This exercise is for those who have to some degree already cultivated the sense of awareness described above. The exercise is best performed as a passenger in a moving vehicle of some sort. The passenger seat of an automobile is the ideal place to do it because of the all-over view afforded. DO NOT do this exercise while driving. The goal of this exercise is to move you out of the "identification" stage—which is only a crutch, a tool to get you to the place where you can perform an exercise such as this—and into the stage of simply experiencing, but experiencing in a more conscious way.

Look—really look—at what you are passing by or sitting in the middle of: other cars, the sides of the road, bicyclists, pedestrians, anything that would affect your driving if you were driving. See. Do not let other thoughts intrude.

If you find yourself looking at these things, but thinking of *other* things (like where you have to be, how slowly the traffic is moving, how late you are, etc.), then you are not *seeing*, you are only looking. To remedy this situation, begin to describe the things you are looking at to yourself. In a traffic jam, where things are not moving all that quickly, it may be necessary to go into great detail about the things you are looking at. You will probably notice things you would never have noticed otherwise. You are beginning to see.

If, on the other hand, you are being carried along quite quickly it will probably be all you can do just to see what you are seeing. So just see. Never mind trying to identify anything; identifying is just a way to keep your mind from wandering, a way to get it used to paying attention. Only identify or describe to yourself if you suddenly find that you're thinking about something that isn't what you're looking at. In other words, only identify things if you discover yourself to be *looking* instead of *seeing*.

Advanced Driving Exercise

Very few people enjoy being stuck in traffic (although I can promise you that having a bottle of bubble-blowing solution at the ready makes a big difference in that situation), but it may just be possible that at least some degree of traffic control lies in the minds of the drivers on the road.

Let's take a step back to the over-used phrase "creating reality." The New Age message that "you create your own reality" is widely misunderstood and might have been at least a little more clearly rendered as "*we* create *our* own reality." None of us lives in a vacuum. Reality, as we know it, is constant, massive *co*-creation. It really does take two ... or more ... to tango.

On any given day, on any given major highway, countless thousands of people may be traveling, each of them carrying with them their own personal vibration, drawing to them the experiences they need. Among those experiences may be having an accident, being stuck for hours, breaking down, whatever. If you are sharing the road with that person, you and your vibrational field apparently need to be there. So there's that.

Then there's your very good mind and what goes on in there, and if you are a person who is paying attention to things, if you are a person who is cultivating awareness, then you likely also have a nice, big, comfy, infectious (and I mean that in the nicest way) auric field ... that people are driving through because that's what we do. The vast majority of us have auras that extend out a whole lot farther than we realize. I was once told that the auric field of the average person extends out for about a mile if it is uncontrolled. Exercising control, you can draw your aura way in closer but without your consciousness attending it, our auric fields are pretty much constantly intermingling, often with folks we don't even know ... which is what happens on the road.

So, here's you and your aura and your awareness, all alert, out for a road trip. Normally—at least normally for the alert, aware, conscious person that you are—your eyes are engaged in assessing road conditions, the status of cars around you, the periphery of the highway; your mind is paying attention. Let's take that a step farther into the realm of co-creating a lovely driving experience by allowing your awareness to expand to include sensing the entire flow of traffic.

Each of us has a particular driving style; some of us drive more slowly than others, some drive faster, some hate to pass, others can't abide having a vehicle in front of them. To perform this exercise you first have to become aware of *your* style. It doesn't matter what your style is, but it's important to know what it is because you need to be comfortable with other people's responses to it; you have to be completely fine with people passing you or with people who drive so slowly that you feel as if you must pass them. In other words, you must allow for the driving behavior both of yourself and everyone on the road, passing no judgments, feeling no anxieties, no anger. You must be at peace.

That in itself may be an exercise for some, but once you've got it down, you are ready to proceed to the second stage of the exercise, which consists, first, of planting yourself at a safe driving distance behind someone of your own style, someone that you can feel comfortable having in front of you. Once there, enlarge the distance between you a little, small enough so that no one would want to slip in, yet large enough to allow plenty of play in your response time should a sudden stop occur.

Become conscious of that space and of the harmony into which you have entered, then extend that consciousness to your peripheral vision so that you are, as moments go by, fully aware of yourself, your position in relation to the vehicle in front of you, the road, your surroundings and—peripherally—what is going on in them. This may sound like a lot, but if you drive, you are already doing it, at least to some extent, you are just not aware that you are doing it; that awareness is what your consciousness is bringing to this exercise.

Your surroundings include what you see peripherally, what you see in front of you, and what you see from the rear-view mirrors. At first, you will need to have silence to bring all of this to a state of full consciousness, but once you are able to do that, you will also be able to passively listen to the radio or to CDs. You cannot engage in conversation, either with a passenger or on the phone as that makes external demands on your conscious mind that will, per force, distract you from this enhanced driving mode.

Now, pay close attention to the space you are keeping between your vehicle and the one in front of you; keep that space regular. Most drivers brake (pretty much unconsciously) for a variety of unnecessary reasons; usually it's something they've just spotted, because they have not been maintaining the kind of pan-awareness that I've been describing. The end result of mindless braking is the sort of traffic that one usually encounters on major highways, choppy and inconsistent, with a lot of lane changing. If you maintain the optimal space between you and the person in front of you, when that driver hits the brake for a fraction of a second, all you need do is remove your foot from the gas pedal. In another fraction of a second that driver will be hitting the gas again, at which point you can too.

In doing this, you begin to affect the flow of traffic around you; the cars behind you will not, in knee-jerk fashion, hit their brakes. They, too, will automatically—and unconsciously—allow their car to slow, thereby sustaining more of a flow in the traffic that is behind you, some of which will eventually pass you, unless you are the fastest person on the road, and they will carry with them a slightly altered, somewhat more relaxed approach to their driving. On a very long trip, you will find that after about thirty minutes of doing this, traffic will seem strangely smooth. Even areas that are known to produce serious back-ups will move with more regularity ... I have actually experienced serious miles-long back-ups weaken and dissolve as I have sat, patiently holding a nice space between myself and the car in front of me as we, at first, inch along. Then as if by magic, despite the blinking warning signs on the overpasses, everything begins moving quite smoothly, slowly at first, but then it quickly returns to completely normal.

I cannot explain why this happens. I only know, from experience, that it does. However, it makes logical sense to me as traffic analysis has studied and identified that traffic moves in very predictable and rather organic ways and that something as seemingly innocuous as an accident pulled off to the side of a road can affect traffic for many hours after it occurs, long after it has been cleared away. I saw no reason why the converse might not be true as well, which is why I began experimenting with it. It seems to me to be equally provable should some traffic researcher wish to study it.

The mind is useful as a tool, helpful to bring you back on track when you catch yourself thinking about extraneous things when you should be focused on driving but when the mind is driving you and you are driving the car, nothing exceptional is happening.

The more you do this, the more you will be able to see and the more aware you'll become. You will begin to notice automatically things you would not have seen before. This is because you will have learned, by doing, to focus your concentration on seeing rather than wasting your energy, assessing. The only concern of your mind will be taking in visual information. You will find that this is a very relaxing thing to do once you learn to do it properly. It clears the mind while you are involved in very ordinary circumstances.

Although other exercises in this book deal precisely with things going on in your mind *while* you are looking at things, your mind needs to be relaxed and free from outside interference in order to allow this to happen. You cannot adequately guide your mind in a mental exercise while it is trying to figure out this month's budget. The following exercises are designed to strengthen your connection with the Spirit that is your driving force, and they will train you to eliminate extraneous material from your mind so that it can tend to the business of reconnecting you to the life you are living.

Acceptance

The more you are able to settle into a deep trust and patience with the rhythm of your own life, the more your heart will open and the softer and the more yielding you will become in your attitude to everything and everyone that comes your way.

—Richard Rudd, *Gene Keys*

It is not what happens to us that determines how our lives will be, but how we respond to what happens to us, so we have to be alert to the responses and reactions that we have ... that is why, where personal growth is concerned, awareness matters, but there's more to acquiring the kind of equanimity that creates you as a peaceful being able to transmit clear energy.

Spirit is in charge of this show; I've mentioned this before. Mind is in charge of cataloging information that needs to be available for any number of purposes. Body houses both Spirit and Mind though the body actually *generates* mind since that function—what we call thinking—is the result of the activity of the brain and the brain is an organ of the body. Mind would have no reason for being were it not for Body, which would have no reason for being were it not for Spirit, hence Spirit is the jumping-off point for everything about the life experiences that we have.

Spirit makes all the decisions about this life that we experience. Spirit doesn't make mistakes. So it's up to us to get used to that ... and it can take some getting used to.

You've probably heard it said that we are never given anything that we can't handle, and it's quite possible that you've heard it either when you were at the end of your rope or you were talking to someone who was at the end of theirs and were reminding themselves of that. And it's true. It's true precisely because Spirit doesn't make mistakes.

You might think about life in terms of this extended metaphor: a game in which Spirit takes on, as its playing piece, a vehicle (a human body) that is both impermanent and flawed, that has been pieced together from various components of other game pieces (DNA), some of which are no longer even in the game and that has been preprogrammed to respond to life in ways that may or may not be contrary to the ways that a particular Spirit would choose to approach the game. Spirit's challenge, then, is to rework its playing piece (your body and the mind it generates) from the inside, out by attempting to establish a respectful form of communication with it. Who you think you are is no more than a fabrication of the mind that the brain has generated, an idea of a self.

Accepting this premise is one of the keys to being able, ultimately, to enjoy being alive. Learning to come to terms with the body you have, even more importantly, learning to love it, is what will help you help others to do the same. There can be no real healing unless there is love inside you.

Allowing

Fishermen go out to sea with hooks and lines and nets and traps; sometimes they have a good day and sometimes they don't. Whales that consume baleen, fish so small you can barely see them, just open their mouths and swim and get all the food they need, every day. Some people go out into the world armed with plans and schemes, some with litanies of affirmations or prayers; sometimes they get what they need, and sometimes they don't. There are other people, though, who go out into the world with their hearts and their minds open; they go with the flow and they find that everything that they need comes to them.

Daily Meditations and Disciplines

A Menu

Pick what suits you, mix and match to design your own.

The following piece, which I call The Gift, was developed in meditation over a period of months. It is designed to balance, refresh, and rejuvenate the entire interdimensional energetic and physical being. It is also a healing in itself and can be "prescribed" for someone needing healing on a daily basis.

I urge you to use this piece, or something like it, every day to reconnect yourself to the all-encompassing and eternal Divine energy of which you are a part and which energy keeps you a vibrant source of healing energy for others. Or use it as an inspiration for creating your own meditational piece that you can use every day. Life is a series of overlapping patterns. As you establish your own pattern in your life the Universe will support you in maintaining it.

First Discipline—The Gift

Allow yourself to see, feel, or be conscious of all that follows. When possible, move as you feel directed to move in response to the energies moving through you ... when you move and vocalize at the same time your body integrates information at a deeper level.

I bind myself this day to the power of the Ocean, the swiftness of the Wind, the endurance of the Earth, the fiery energy of the Sun, the gentle and regular cycles of the Moon and Stars, the eternal cycling of the DNA, this perfect body, the spoken word, the sound of silence, and all the Love in the Universe. [*Using your arms and hands, draw the Love into your heart or heart chakra.*]

I call out now for a Pillar of Light to move through the Physical, Energetic, and Spiritual Bodies to clear all the energy centers of all my bodies, both known and unknown. [*Raise your hands above your head in an open wide, receiving gesture and beam through yourself, toward Earth as you speak.*]

I call out now for that Pillar of Light to move through the Physical, Energetic, and Spiritual Bodies to replenish, rejuvenate, and activate all the energy centers of my bodies, both known and unknown. [*Repeat same action as previous.*]

I draw up the energy of my Mother, the Earth, to invigorate and rejuvenate this physical body. [*Use the hands to draw up the energy.*]

I draw down the energy of the Divine to invigorate and rejuvenate the Spirit that dwells within this Sacred Body. [*Use the hands to draw down the energy.*]

I draw up the energy of the Earth to anchor this body strongly to the Earth from which it comes. [*Draw the energy up and clasp hands over the lower belly to anchor the energy into the lower three chakras.*]

I draw down the energy of the Divine to anchor this Spirit to the Divine from which it comes. [*Draw down the energy into the third eye, throat, and heart chakras to anchor.*]

Firmly grounded Spiritually and Physically, I call for the release from every level of my Being of any and all misqualified energies or energies of lack, into the Violet Transmuting Flame that surrounds my body that those energies may be transmuted into Golden Healing Light.

I call for this brilliant, clarified Golden Light to be returned to me, at every level of my Being, in every dimension in which this Being exists, for my edification and education.

[*Cross arms over the chest and open when releasing, draw back in again when pulling the Light in.*]

[*Now, holding the hands in the auric field around the head, feet planted firmly on the ground, about shoulder width apart.*] I call now for the perfect balance and alignment of the Brain, the Central Nervous System, the Pineal and the Pituitary Glands allowing my Light Body to perfectly align with my Physical Body.

[*Maintain hands in same position.*]

I call now for the perfect balance and alignment of **all** Energetic and Spiritual Bodies that surround this Physical Body—higher and lower, inner and outer, known and unknown. [*Open your arms out into your energy bodies as you speak, then embrace yourself, breathing all these balanced energies into you. Known bodies may be named, if desired.*]

[*Now hold hands out and down, beaming toward the Earth.*] I call out now to the cellular consciousness of this Physical Body to release and return to my Mother, the Earth any and all energies which are no longer serving Life within this Physical Body. I call out to her NOW to replenish, restore, and rejuvenate this Physical Body with whatever Energies from the Earth may be required to perfectly balance and align this Physical Body at this moment, NOW.

[*Draw hands in to the belly/navel area and breathe in deeply.*]

And now, in the name of the Divine [*or Jesus, Buddha, God/Goddess, etc., whatever appeals to you*], my own True Self, I call out to the I AM Presence and to the Angel of that Presence to draw in from the Universe any and all information and energies that may be needed to activate, rejuvenate, replenish, and restore the DNA of the many bodies which I AM to a state that will perfectly support the Light Being which I AM becoming.

In my Perfected Condition, totally connected to my Mother, the Earth and to my Father, the Divine I call out to the Spirit of my Being and to my Higher Self to align in absolute perfection and consciousness with my waking, conscious mind to guide me through this day.

With my Entire Being now filled with Divine Love and Light I send my gratitude for this Physical Body to my Mother, the Earth. And for allowing me this remarkable experience of Life on Earth I send my gratitude to my Father, the Divine. I send my gratitude also to this physical body for the job it has done in carrying out the will of the Spirit and I rejoice in this life and in my being.

THANK YOU!

Now, take some time to connect with and thank all teachers and guides of any sort that you may work with throughout the day. If you have been asked to send healing to others, connect with the Divine Love in your heart and send Love as a supporting energy to the Angels or Higher Selves of those you wish to support. Simply see the recipients of that Love in a Perfect State of Being and know that this state is available to them should they wish to embrace it.

The Gift, as I have presented it here, is in its original form. As I practice it for myself today, it is different having been added to, subtracted from, and adjusted as necessary, as I have shifted and grown. What we need to support us changes as we change and grow. So again, I stress, The Gift is a jumping-off point. Make it your own or make your own, add to it or subtract from it, but do it every day until it simply becomes you.

Pillar of Light Exercise

Pronounciation Guide

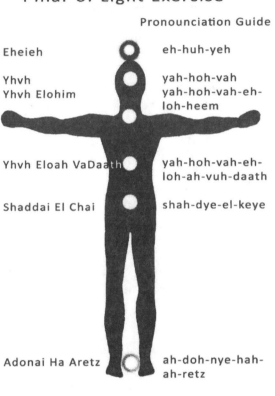

Eheieh	eh-huh-yeh
Yhvh	yah-hoh-vah
Yhvh Elohim	yah-hoh-vah-eh-loh-heem
Yhvh Eloah VaDaath	yah-hoh-vah-eh-loh-ah-vuh-daath
Shaddai El Chai	shah-dye-el-keye
Adonai Ha Aretz	ah-doh-nye-hah-ah-retz

with many thanks to Ted Andrews

Another nice integrating exercise is the Pillar (or Tower) of Light, which I've borrowed from Ted Andrews, who borrowed it from someone else, who borrowed it from someone else, and so on and so on.

First, picture a pillar of light descending from the sky toward the top of your head. Recite each of the words listed on the illustration (see figure) while focusing on that part of your body with which the word is pictured. Start at the crown, drawing the light down through your body and into the earth, reciting as you go.

I did this exercise aloud, too, chanting the words. It felt a little weird at first, but the energetic feel of the tones resonating in my body was so wonderful that I got hooked. You can do this five to nine times if you like. I found that three times were sufficient for me when I first began using this exercise. After a couple of years, one time was all that felt necessary. It has, by now, become a part of me.

When you get done chanting, breathe and see or visualize your breath arising from the earth, coming up through the center of your body and out the top of your head, surrounding you with light. Ted suggested picturing this happening four times front and back and four times side to side. I have found that doing it three times while envisioning a total sphere of light surrounding my body suits me better. Sometimes I see the light as golden; sometimes I see it as sparkles. It changes from day to day. I'm not sure why it changes but I love the variety! I recommend starting with Ted's original exercise and see where it takes you.

For the Goddess oriented, the following piece by Abby Willowroot will do nicely:

A Healing Chant

Deep in my Bones
The Goddess is alive
Deep in my cells and blood
The Life Force is strong
Deep in my heart and spirit
I believe I will heal
I feel the Goddess at my core
Filling me with faith and health
Abundant Life Forces of the Universe
Flow in me, and banish all disease
My blood, my bones, my cells and my body
Are healing now, are healing now
The Goddess force is in me
And healing me now

Second Discipline

If you want to provide healing energy on a consistent basis, use it every day either on yourself or on someone else. (Or some*thing* else ... plants, crystals, pets, appliances, cars, whatever! I once "healed" a rather large piece of equipment.) The same rule applies to healing skills as applies to muscles in the body: the more you use them, the stronger they will get. The power and the ability to channel Divine Energy, should you fail to exercise it on a daily basis, will never actually go away, it will just get weaker and weaker and weaker as time passes. A very active practitioner, one who is using their skills on a number of people every day, though, is encouraged to take a day or two off every once in a while! Vacationing is not just good, but necessary for the soul.

Third Discipline

Spend at least a few fully conscious minutes outdoors if you can, breathing in all the aspects of the day (air, masculine). Imagine the energy of the earth (feminine) flowing into your body through the chakras of your feet. Open your arms to the breeze and the sunlight (fire), letting their (masculine) energies flow into your body. If it's raining or snowing, it's easy to incorporate the energy of water (feminine) into your being. If water isn't present where you are, just hold out your hands, palms down toward the earth, and call upon the flow of the waters beneath the earth to nourish you. Scientists have recently learned that there are even rocks that have water within them.

Of course, in really inclement weather or emergency circumstances you can do all this indoors on the pure strength of your intent. Performing the ritual outside just felt more satisfying to me. Having a window to gaze out of can be enough if you are inside and running water or a fountain, a candle, the floor beneath your feet, and the air in your home will do just fine when necessary.

If you really want to empower your day, call upon the angelic elements to assist you. Quiet yourself and, if you have any Beings who assist you, thank them for their assistance. Then ask that they help you to send Divine Energy into every aspect of your day. List the activities you will be involved in and beam Divine Energy through your hands out in front of you as though you were (because you are!) sending energy through your body, out into your day. This is an extremely effective way to get the most out of your day.

Fourth Discipline

Listen closely to your body.

This may take some practice as you may have been raised to listen to what everybody else told you was good for your body. This usually starts when you are a child, with your immediate family telling you what to eat and when to eat. Now is the time to set aside those old rules in order to be able to listen to your body and to its wisdom!

Your body knows what is good for it, and it sends you subtle messages all the time ... and it sends not-so-subtle messages if you haven't been listening to it. One way to get to know your body is to fast for a couple of days and then introduce a new food at the rate of one a day (or one a meal, if you're feeling particularly confident or are desperate for a new taste in your mouth). Note your body's responses to each new food that you add. Note how satisfied—or dissatisfied—you feel, how comfortable or uncomfortable your body feels. You may even want to keep a journal of the process while you're doing it to enhance your full awareness of the experience. You may also want to throw the journal out when you're done, unless you're writing an article on your experiences or are doing this exercise as some sort of research project. The process is nothing to obsess over; it's just a way to develop the habit of listening to your body so that you know what is truly nourishing for it and for you.

Nourishment is about more than providing vitamins, minerals, fiber, and fluids; it is also about providing a deep sense of satisfaction, an emotionally palpable experience of the sensual pleasure of eating and drinking. Our bodies are designed to feel good; eating and drinking are, at their best, emotionally gratifying experiences. In fact, sometimes we may need to eat a very specific thing precisely because it fulfills an emotional need that can be physically triggered.

Chocolate is famously known for this! As long as the action—the consuming—is done consciously, it can be a good and a healthy thing.

Your body's needs change over time: pay attention. I spent years during my healing process as a vegetarian but when my body got better it wanted—*needed*—some animal protein. As you change, the needs of your body change too. It's critical to your well-being to follow the dictates of your body. It is lovely not to *need* animal protein but if your body needs it—and some genetic types function better with it—find what your body responds well to and eat it. Be conscious of exactly what is going on, give thanks to the creature in question. Respect your body by giving it what it needs to function well.

Until I was in my forties I couldn't even taste tofu; now I actually crave it sometimes. If you don't listen to your body, you'll never find out what it needs. Eat what your body tells you is good for it no matter what you may read or hear about a given food. Everybody's body chemistry is different, and very few pieces of information apply equally to everyone. The most important things, where food is concerned, are to be conscious of what you are eating, to be conscious of where it came from, and to be in a pleasant mood while you are eating it. Give thanks and enjoy!

If you feel "logey" (an amazing word! It means curiously sluggish and maybe even a little stiff), then your body wants to move. Do it! Don't let your body down. Exercise is different for everybody too. Very often people who run up and down stairs when they could walk, or walk to the store when they could drive, don't ever get logey and so don't need any more exercise. But all bodies, even ones that are confined to wheelchairs, need some movement. Moving the external body stimulates the organs inside and that is especially critical to the processing of food.

Sunrise Salute

A simple and easy way to add motion to your body and energy to your internal organs is to start your day off with an uneven number of repetitions of the Sunrise Salute, an ancient series of yoga poses that was designed to stimulate every organ in the body. It is meant to be done at a fairly quick pace, unlike regular yoga poses, which are frequently held for minutes at a time. The entire Sunrise Salute is considered as one pose; it takes about a minute to go through one series. (See figure for the poses that make up the Sunrise Salute.)

The "uneven number" requirement is made because numbers, like everything else, carry vibration. Uneven numbers are dynamic, and since the Sunrise Salute is designed to activate all of the internal systems of the body, dynamism is appropriate. (Even numbers bring stability.)

Your body is not only the temple for your spirit (and it should be honored as such), but it is also a valuable and sensitive tool for the transmission of energy. It requires very good care.

There is one foolproof way to become more deeply in touch not only with your body but with your soul and your spirit's desires as well: Sleep Magic. Sleep Magic performed on a regular basis allows you to build better communication between you and your body and, by extension, between you, your soul, and your spirit. (See the last few pages of this book for a taste of the technique.)

Fifth Discipline

Drink lots and lots of water—pure water—not tea, not juice, water. If you have not consumed at least a quart of water in a day, you probably haven't had enough. Channeling energy demands that the body be well hydrated. Although you do not absorb physical toxins from those you work on, other toxins do pass through your body. It needs to be cleansed so that it can be an unimpeded vehicle through which energy can pass. (There is such a thing as taking in too much water. If you are not in an area that is exceedingly hot and dry and you are drinking more than a gallon a day, it might bear looking into.)

Sixth Discipline

If you are doing healing work, cleanse yourself regularly using the energy of the elements themselves. Washing your hands the "normal" way counts, just be conscious of the release that is taking place to further empower it. The following are some out-of-the-ordinary—and deeper—methods of elemental cleansing.

1. Standing on the earth if you can, barefoot if you can, with your palms parallel to the earth, ask your Mother Earth to take from you all that no longer benefits you (and that no longer benefits the client or clients you have most recently worked on), but which feeds Her. Then ask that the areas vacated by that energy be filled with her healing light and love.

2. With arms outstretched, preferably outdoors, ask that Grandfather Air take from you all that no longer benefits you or your clients, but which empowers and enlivens Him. Then ask that He fill the empty spaces created by this with His light and love.

3. With palms facing the sun (or a flame) ask that Father Fire take from you all that no longer benefits you or your clients, but which feeds and nourishes Him. Then ask for the empty spaces created by that to be filled with His healing light and love.

4. With hands in running water ask Grandmother Water to take from you all that no longer benefits you or your clients, but which nourishes Her and ask that those empty spaces be filled with Her light and love.

Feel free to call upon the elements as they relate to you: father, mother, cousin, uncle, whatever. Or don't call them anything at all ... just call them! It is your relationship with them that is important, not what you call them.

At one point in my life, for purposes of my own healing, and before I had opened to unconditional forgiveness and love, I chose new parents and grandparents for myself and they were the elements. If you come from a background that has provided you with less than nurturing relatives, you may wish to replace your biological relatives with elemental relatives. I loved my new family and felt both loved and supported enough by them to advance into forgiveness and, ultimately, love for the people who helped create the challenges that created me as I am.

Cleansing in each of the individual elements deepens your relationship and interaction with them and their relationship and interaction with you. It is a symbiotic relationship; everyone gains from it. The process needs to be done and cannot be taken for granted. Both your body and the elements with which you are working need to be respected and honored. The elements need energetic nourishment every bit as much as you do. It has been our neglect of nourishing the elements that has left us in poor relationship with our Mother Earth.

A handy time to cleanse is when you are showering or washing at the end of the day. It allows you to cleanse on two levels, the physical and the spiritual. This is basic maintenance, not an overnight "cure," but the results, if used faithfully over time, are impressive. I always thank Fire for heating the water, Water for carrying off all the energies I no longer have a use for, Air for its life-giving oxygen, and Earth for her constant support of me. Then I envision all the day's energies washing away with the water as it goes down the drain. This transformative practice works for anyone, not just lightworkers! Share it with your friends!

Doing the Work

A Word about Protection

We live in a fear-based society; even some of our lightworkers are running scared. Information abounds on how to "protect yourself" when you are doing healing work. Each morning when I fill myself with sunlight I know—I simply but strongly *know*—that I am Divine Light. And, guess what, I AM ... and so are you.

There are two sets of extremely powerful words, with which you can make anything happen. They are "I AM" and "I WILL." When your body is cleared of contrary-wise programming and you intend strongly, with emotion, using either of those phrases, the result is manifestation. So do not be afraid to work on anyone, ever. **Know** that you ARE the infinite light and love of the Divine Universe and nothing will ever penetrate your energetic field. It will not be able to.

The Knowing I speak of is cell-deep knowing, not something that is generated by your mind. The mind, as we know, can be both powerful and helpful but it is, after all, generated by the cells of the brain, cells that have been programmed since before you were even born. If anything in that programming exists that even suggests doubt, it will compromise Knowingness and it will take many years of so-called positive thought to change it because it takes the human body seven years to turn over all its cells on its own. Certain forms of energy psychology, such as Sleep Magic and EMDR (Eye Movement Desensitization and Reprocessing) can speed the process up by lightening the load your cells carry and allowing you to *feel* clear, but your body will not be physically cleared for at least seven years because that is the nature of the body. If you know that you carry a certain level of doubt, I'd suggest that you investigate those options.

Incidentally, if you are ever asked to beam protective light to someone else, do them a favor and beam them golden light. White light is the best for clearing and harmonizing but golden works better for protection.

All of the previous exercises and rituals have been designed to assist you in creating yourself as a calm, centered, grounded human being through which clear energy can flow easily and efficiently, allowing you to provide for others what they may not be able to provide for themselves: unqualified healing energy. Fully awake, fully aware, and as conscious as you can be, you have the ability to tune in to the vibrations of others more easily and without judgment; you have the ability to be the best human being—and healer—that you can be.

Beginning a Treatment

(I will, for the duration of this segment be switching back and forth between using "him," "her," "their," "she," "he," and "them" for purpose of gender balance.)

Prior to any treatment you should, of course, make sure that your hands are clean and that your mind is at peace. Ideally your client should recline to receive a treatment in the most relaxed way. If it is necessary that your client is seated (for instance, he may be in a wheelchair or in a situation where reclining is not an option), make sure that he is as comfortable as possible. While you are working on him, attend closely to your own posture and comfort also, so that you do not become uncomfortable or hurt yourself in the process of making him feel better! If you are unable to reach areas of the back because your client is seated, either place your hands on the back of the chair and project through it, or align your hands as closely as possible along his sides and project in from there. Intention will always get the energy where it needs to go, but there is a certain comfort provided for your client when he feels your hands in what he senses are the "right places."

When your client is reclining it is most usual for a treatment to occur with him lying on his back. Psychologically there are many very obvious reasons for this, especially when you are with someone who is new to you. Establishing trust is the first and most important reason, and being able to see you at work helps to establish this trust. But there may be times when it is essential or simply preferred (his back hurts!) that you begin a treatment with your client lying face down. A woman in the later stages of pregnancy will need to lie on one side or the other. Just make sure she, her spine, and her belly are comfortable and supported.

In all cases, the first thing you must attend to is the physical comfort of your client. Does he need extra support under the knees, ankles, or neck? Is the temperature comfortable for him? Always assure your client that he may speak to you at any time, either to ask questions or to ensure that he is comfortable. Many people, unacquainted with energy work, feel "trapped" in a quasi-magical state where they sense that they are not supposed to speak. Needless to say this does not add to their sense of comfort or their ability to relax.

The second thing you must do is ground yourself. There are a wide variety of ways to ground yourself, ranging from dropping an energetic cord from your navel down into the core of the earth, to imagining that your feet have grown roots. Any method that plants you firmly in the energy of the earth will do. So do whatever works for you; just don't forget to do it.

Then make sure that your client understands the way you work. If you are going to lay your hands on someone, let them know so that they are not startled. Ours is a touch-deprived society and most people who need healing also need safe touch. Healing energy can be transferred either in the auric fields surrounding the body or in a hands-on fashion. I use both methods depending on the situation, but I rely heavily on hands-on work. If you will be working solely in the auric field make sure that your client understands, as much as that is possible, how it happens that you can send them healing energy without ever touching them.

Healing in the auric field and hands-on healing are equally effective. You just need to let your client know what you are doing so that he or she can be comfortable. Knowing is always more comfortable than not knowing, and a person who is comfortable will be more receptive to the energy you are providing.

The next thing that must be done is to open yourself to the source of the energy with which you are working. Those trained in Reiki often choose to use the standard kanji positions (special hand positions used in Reiki to connect with Earth energy), but that is not necessary. When I performed Reiki attunements, I never taught kanji positions because all you need do to open yourself to Divine Energy is to ask the Universe that you be an open, clear channel for Divine Light (Divine Love, Divine Energy, or however you like to verbally connect with All That Is) and it happens. A sense of knowingness or a feeling will overtake you. I imagine that this sense or feeling could be completely different for everyone. I definitely *feel* it but some people feel nothing. It is not the feeling that matters; it is the *knowing*. Either way the connection happens immediately, the moment you ask for it. You can know with certainty that if you have asked, you have received. You are connected.

If desired, you can call upon Jesus or any other teacher, guide, or Master with whom you would like to work to assist you in transmitting energy. You can also call upon your angel or angels, or any other deities or energies that work with you at this point, although this can also be done at any point in the treatment. You may do this silently or aloud as the situation demands or as your comfort level allows.

Then briefly cup your hands out in front of you over the heart chakra of your client, at your own heart level. Visualize your hands being filled with shining light. Then turn your palms down, toward your client, and radiate that light into her.

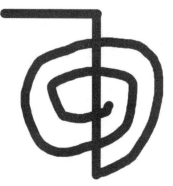

You may also want to draw the Cho Ku Rei symbol at this point if you feel that you need added power. (Cho Ku Rei is a symbol used both in and outside of Reiki to amplify energy. You may use it at any point in a treatment for added oomph! Refer to the drawing preceding this paragraph for an example.)

Now you are ready to begin.

You will usually begin working at the head to ensure that your client's mind is in a calm, receptive state. If you can sense/feel that your client's mind is not in a clear/receptive state, simply allow the peace that is within you to flow through your hands into your client as you hold their head in your energetic field.

Whether you work with your hands directly on the head or in the auric field surrounding it, the head is where you will get an overall feel for your client's energy and a smooth entry into her energetic field. The crown chakra (just off the body at the very top of the head) is the chakra that is the connection between body and Spirit, and is where the highest vibrational level of energy usually resides.

The third eye, sometimes known as the pineal chakra, sits in the forehead just above and between the eyes; its vibrational level is also very high. After you feel that the client has relaxed, begin by moving your hands about the person's head, close to, but not touching, it. See how your hands feel as they move over different areas. When you get to a spot that seems to call out to you (This is an indescribable sensation that may manifest as a feeling of coldness, warmth, or tingling or simply as a *knowing*. You'll understand it when you sense it for yourself. It is different for everyone.), place your hands on (or in, if you're working in the auric field) the spot and allow yourself to become aware of the other person's energy.

Allow your focus to become soft.

Stop thinking.

Feel.

Thus begins the co-creation of the treatment that is about to occur. Whenever two people (or more) are involved there is always co-creation. A healing is not you making something happen; it is you providing energy for someone else to make something happen. The energy you are providing is not yours, and the end result is not yours. Remind yourself of this on a regular basis.

The energy you are providing is not yours, and the end result is not yours.

57

The Chakras, One by One

The Seventh Chakra: The Crown Chakra, Sahasrara

(Violet/White/Gold)

(The traditional colors of the chakras have been with us for thousands of years. These colors began to shift hundreds of years ago with the result that you will now see some of the chakras listed as having more than one color associated with them. The color shifts are occurring because the vibrational field of the earth has been changing and will continue to change.)

The crown chakra is just above and barely touching the top of the head; how much of the top of the head it covers depends on the person on whom you are working. The whole head will be happy for all the attention you can give it. The pineal gland, the pituitary gland, the amygdala, the Alta Major (which mitigates the reception of Light for interdimensional communication and is located at the back of the head), the primary sensory receptors for taste, smell, vision, and hearing are all in the head, as are the sinuses, the brain, and the third eye.

There is a high concentration of focal areas on the head and plenty to work on. If your client has an area of particular interest make sure to acknowledge her concern by working directly on that area, placing your hands there or stating your intent to work on that area. Energy goes where it needs to, but your client may not know that and your reassurance of direct touch or a spoken intent can be comforting. If her area of interest is on the back of her head, assure her that the energy will go there or slide your hand beneath her head if it is comfortable for both of you.

Let your intuition, the direction of your guides or angels, or the direction of your client's guides or angels, inform the placement of your hands. If your client lives with a great deal of stress, has high blood pressure, or is going through a period of major transformation, be sure to attend to the brain itself. Set your intention on the holographic instruction of the brain (a process in which the brain learns new energy patterns in a holistic way, integrating all the information at once), and beam energy inward. Unless you feel an imbalance or a need to send extra energy to one place in particular, keep your hands in a balanced formation on either side of the brain and let the energy flow evenly back and forth between your hands.

Cover the brain evenly. Divine Energy is wonderfully stimulating for the seventh chakra. You can spend a whole session just working on someone's brain! It's great before exams and during especially stressful situations!

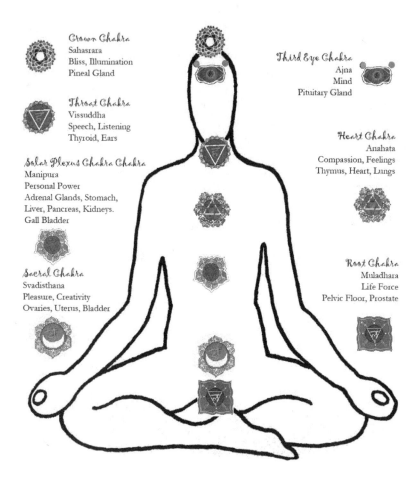

Crown Chakra
Sahasrara
Bliss, Illumination
Pineal Gland

Third Eye Chakra
Ajna
Mind
Pituitary Gland

Throat Chakra
Vissuddha
Speech, Listening
Thyroid, Ears

Heart Chakra
Anahata
Compassion, Feelings
Thymus, Heart, Lungs

Solar Plexus Chakra Chakra
Manipura
Personal Power
Adrenal Glands, Stomach,
Liver, Pancreas, Kidneys.
Gall Bladder

Sacral Chakra
Svadisthana
Pleasure, Creativity
Ovaries, Uterus, Bladder

Root Chakra
Muladhara
Life Force
Pelvic Floor, Prostate

The crown chakra itself is not usually a trouble spot because it is our connection with All That Is, and all of us have that connection simply by being alive. However, what you may find is that the crown chakra may not be in right relation to the chakras below it. So, as you move to lower and lower chakras, take a moment to rest one hand on the lower chakra, and the other hand, briefly, on the crown. If you feel an energetic connection (for me it's a little like the feeling of holding either end of a Slinky® toy), then you can continue working on the lower chakra. If, on the other hand, your client's energy feels "dead" in between your hands, let your hands rest in place until you feel, sense, or know that a connection has developed between the two chakras. The natural balance for the crown chakra is the root chakra. If you imagine the heart chakra to be like the pivot of a seesaw, you might imagine three chakras on either side of it, balancing each other: 1 balancing 7, 2 balancing 6, and 3 balancing 5. (The Heart Chakra (3) and the Crown (7) should, additionally, balance with each of the other chakras.)

Refer to the illustration preceding this paragraph as a reference for chakra locations.

The Sixth Chakra: The Third Eye Chakra, Ajna

(Violet/Indigo/Yellow)

Located in the forehead, between the eyes, the third eye is the center of clairvoyance, clear dreaming, visions, and the wisdom to move spiritual information into the physical realm. It is the eye of your Higher Self.

Especially in cases where there are second chakra issues (cysts, tumors, any ovarian or uterine disturbances), test the balance between the sacral plexus (the second chakra) and the third eye. If the balance feels uneven, allow the energy flowing through you to restore it to a state of equilibrium.

The Fifth Chakra: The Throat or Neck Chakra, Visshuddha

(Sky Blue/Silver)

The throat can be a difficult area to lay your hands on directly, especially if the person on whom you are working is either very heavy or very small. Often it is easiest and most comfortable for your client if you simply cup your hands between his jawbone and collarbone. If it is absolutely essential that your palm chakras contact the surface of the neck directly, place a small pillow, rolled cloth, or towel under the neck so that the head can drop back and your client can remain comfortable. Make sure to remove the prop when you finish in that area unless the client prefers it because the neck is a highly charged emotional area and leaving it exposed or vulnerable can be subconsciously disconcerting, causing your client to become guarded. Being guarded will lessen her relaxation and, as a result, decrease the efficacy of the treatment. The more relaxed the client, the more easily the energy is received.

Besides being the vibratory vehicle for voice to be heard in the world, the neck also houses the thyroid and parathyroid glands. A feeling of warmth and security helps these glands (and everything else in the body!) to function at optimum capacity. The energy of the thyroid is often connected to the energy around one's relationship with one's mother.

Check the balance between the throat chakra and the solar plexus and allow it to adjust as necessary. The tendency of the body is to balance, but a variety of factors from stress to illness often prevent that balance from occurring. The energy you are providing allows the body to adjust itself as needed.

The Manifesting Chakras

(Turquoise)

The manifesting chakras have no numerical designation as such. They relate to the ability of the heart chakra to have its desires manifest in the physical world.

The existence and purpose of the manifesting chakras was revealed to me while I was in training during the thirty-day practice period following the Reiki master attunement I received. Beings of Light showed up in my healing room where I was practicing on the very first day and came every day thereafter, repeatedly attuning me as I did practice attunements on what I was calling my Higher Self. I say "what I was calling my Higher Self" on purpose because ... how do I know really? Like most humans I wanted to identify what was happening when what was happening was most certainly not under my control so I gave things names and I felt more comfortable.

The manifesting chakras can be found, left and right on the body, in the slight hollow that forms between the shoulder and the collar bones. Like all the chakras, they radiate out to front, back, and sides more or less like a "ball" of energy.

From the back, the manifesting chakras collect energies while from the front they deal with the capabilities of bringing things into reality. Check the connection between the manifesting chakras and the third eye on someone who is experiencing difficulties making his or her dreams come true.

By resting your hands on the tops of your client's shoulders, just above these chakras, you can discover blocks that may be preventing her from realizing her dreams. Hold the intention of drawing the blocked energy into a dynamic state while your hands are placed directly on each chakra and, when your hands feel full, move them evenly and smoothly down the arms, over the hands, and out the fingers. What you are doing is instructing your client's energetic body on the pathways of manifesting energy. Do this one, three, five, seven, or as many times as you feel is necessary, until you can feel the clear flow of energy through the arm and out the fingertips. (Performing an action an uneven number of times increases dynamism, while performing an action an even number of times adds stability.)

This application is also very helpful in releasing the excess energies that can become trapped in the shoulder from an injury. You may, if that is the case, want to take a moment to balance the manifesting energy by holding one hand on one of the front of the manifesting chakras and the other on your client's palm chakra on the same side of her body. In doing this you are activating her palm chakra to release her productive energy into her world.

One of my teachers, the Reverend Dr. Paula Sunray, once explained that problems with shoulders have their roots in responsibilities that are placed on you while problems with the hips result from responsibilities you have taken on yourself. I have seen this theory validated again and again in my work.

The Thymus

(*Turquoise/Aqua/Sparkles*)

(*The thymus is not a chakra per se but it is a very important and distinct area. It deals not only with the immune system but with interdimensional communication as well.*)

The thymus is located in the center of the chest, slightly above the heart chakra, over the sternum. You may find that this area feels very undeveloped in many people, with not much energy seeming to be gathered there. In that state you are likely to encounter a compromised immune system. When working on acute cases of influenza or other powerful viral infections, the thymus is where your hands will be focusing much energy. The thymus is shaped somewhat like a butterfly. While streaming energy into the thymus, I often visualize the energy from my hands imbuing the thymus/butterfly with golden light and I encourage my clients to do the same.

The Virus Treatment

During the lengthy initiation by the Beings of Light that followed my Reiki master initiation I received the following information about viruses: *That which is known on earth as a viral infection is actually a visitation of another life form whose goal it is to assist in raising the vibrational level of human beings. When a person heals from a viral infection he has not, as is generally perceived, "killed" the virus in his body; he has, rather, integrated the virus into his body and raised his vibrational level.*

Many months later, in the newsletter from the Institute of Noetic Sciences, I came across a small news flash stating that it had been discovered by scientists that viruses were altering the DNA of humans and assisting in the evolution of the species. Viruses may be part of why we no longer resemble our ancient cousins, the Neanderthals. Sleep, vitamin C derived from plant sources, zinc in body-friendly form, goldenseal, echinacea, and animal proteins are all helpful in assisting the body's integration of viruses. There are many other herbs and minerals that can help as well. Individual body chemistry varies greatly from person to person and so will both the products used to produce the best results and the amounts of the products needed to integrate the virus into the system. Find out which products your client may already use and offer suggestions if it seems necessary.

The virus treatment, modified (on instruction) from Kathleen Milner's excellent work in *Reiki and Other Rays of Healing*

Touch, helps the body to integrate viral information and thus raise its vibrational level.

Begin by placing your hands over the manifesting chakras on the front of the body. Let them rest there while you feel the energy build beneath your hands. Then, with only gentle suggestions of hand movement, visualize the Motor-Zanon symbol (Refer to the illustration preceding this paragraph as an example of the symbol.) being drawn beneath each of your hands. Follow this with Cho Ku Ray symbols over each chakra while intoning the word "Motor" (intoning can be done aloud or to yourself) three times. Hold the energy field briefly, then draw both sets of symbols again while intoning the word "Zanon" three times. Continue to hold the energetic field while visualizing the body accepting, absorbing, and adapting to the new data. Feel your client's vibration rise. You may also feel your client's temperature rise. This is a natural response to the integration process. Make sure that you remind your client to drink lots of water for the next day or so!

Upon drawing the first set of symbols, the energy of the Motor-Zanon symbol is taken into the body and the little squiggle in the center spins around, searching out and snagging the virus. When the second set of Motor-Zanon is drawn and the word "Zanon" is intoned, the polarity of the symbol is reversed, and the information carried by the virus is integrated into the body.

After drawing the symbols the first time, you may feel as though it would be helpful to add an extra energy boost to the immune system. If so, place both hands over the thymus and use the image of golden butterfly beneath your hands. You may even ask the recipient to hold the same image. This will assist the body in its process of integration. Then close with the Motor-Zanon symbols on the manifesting chakras. This treatment is very powerful and effective and, if used as soon as a person experiences the first symptoms of the flu or a cold coming on, it can prevent any further symptoms from occurring. Integrating the information releases the necessity for any further inflammation. A case of firmly established flu (one that has clearly taken hold and shows no signs of letting up) may take two or more treatments to integrate.

The virus treatment is a stand-alone treatment and can be completed in ten or fifteen minutes. It is easily done with a seated client and can, therefore, be accomplished in an office setting or any "emergency" location.

The Fourth Chakra: The Heart Chakra, Anahata

(Green/Pink/Red)

While the actual, physical heart sits in the left center of the chest, the heart chakra lies in the exact center. The physical heart is a highly charged area. It is surrounded by, and protected by, the pericardium. The heart is protected because it needs to be; it is very sensitive. As the seat of emotion in the body the heart needs protection from the heavy blows that life can deal out. As a finely tuned electrical device it also needs superior insulation. The pericardium supplies this insulation. In traditional Chinese medicine the heart is a "fire" organ and, as fire is the most energetic of the elements, one does not need to add any more energy to it. This is especially true if the physical heart itself is weak. When there are heart problems, treat the kidneys (which are in charge of distributing the heart's energy through the body) and the thymus, and let the body handle the heart on its own. Use energy only to balance and soothe in the area of the physical heart.

If the lungs are in need of work, as in the case of pneumonia or a severe bronchial infection, place your hands as needed. (NB: a woman's breasts are not considered to be an acceptable place for your hands in a therapeutic situation. Special situations, such as cancers or cysts, can be discussed with your client on an as-needed basis.) In conditions where the lungs are severely compromised, your hands can often feel the very same raspiness that your client feels when breathing. Keep your touch extra gentle if the lungs feel severely compromised.

The general feeling around the heart chakra should be open, expansive, and welcoming. It should feel balanced in relation to all the other chakras. Just as you "weigh" each chakra in relation to the crown chakra, you may wish to do the same in relation to the heart chakra, especially if your client is in an emotionally compromised state.

Balancing the physical heart on the right side of the chest, there is a strongly energetic area that I call the transpersonal heart. While the physical heart concerns itself with emotions and feelings of a personal nature, the transpersonal heart allows us to step outside of the personal into the Universal. It allows us to connect with all other life forms at a very deep level. Run your hand lightly over this area and make sure that it, too, feels open and welcoming. Many women of menopausal age (and the rare man) may tell you of twinges of pain in this area. At this age domestic concerns can be fewer and the soul may broaden its view of and connection with the world at large. In response to this shift in focus the transpersonal heart opens. Sometimes this can be physically experienced as small sharp pains. It is nothing to be concerned about and is quite normal.

The Hand Chakras

In most articles and books on the chakras, you will find the authors writing about the seven largest chakras ... but there are far more chakras than that covering the entire body. I have read, in an old text, that there are 360,000 chakras in the body. If you are the sort of person who enjoys antique books, you may someday run across illustrations depicting a body covered with what appear to be countless chakras.

Americans tend to like things simple and easy, so most modern-day authors stick to the central seven, though some are now recognizing nine large chakras. You have already seen that I don't stick to just the seven large ones. I'm certainly not going to go into all 360,000 of them, but I will devote time to the especially useful ones, like the hand chakras. It's an ever-changing world, and we learn more about ourselves all the time; if you allow your mind and your heart to stay open to possibilities, you will discover much that is useful.

If you are a hands-on healer, then your hand chakras are obvious to you, but for people who are not, even though they can feel the heat from your hands when you touch them, they may never have considered the importance of their own hand chakras ... but look at all the conditions that affect peoples' hands! There's no shortage of them. The blockage or disturbance of the hand chakras is almost always directly tied to the heart chakra in some way. You don't have to know what that way is (though you may find out), you just have to treat it.

Because the hands are so intimately tied to the heart and are also, as a rule, intimately tied to everything we do in the world—since we "do" most things with our hands—blocked hand chakras hint strongly that something, somewhere in that person's life is not in what might be called energetic—or spiritual—integrity. That's enough for you to know. As a hands-on healer, you are not (unless you happen to have been so accredited) a psychotherapist, you are more of a reporter, there to feed back to your client what you feel from the body and to let them know how that condition might be alerting them to inspect some aspect of their life. That inspection need not occur then and there; most healings take time to unfold, especially when the heart is involved.

When the session is complete, and your client is still coming out of the healing trance, gently convey to her that which you have experienced energetically. If the information generates a response that is fine, but it need not, so don't expect one. In fact, it could be helpful to precede your offering of information by suggesting that she just take the information in and "walk with it." "Walk with it" is a phrase that was often used by my first feng shui teacher, Melinda Joy, who had been schooled in Native American ways of healing. Sometimes there is a feeling of urgency to respond when one is given information and sometimes that response can take away from the powerful gift that has been given; "walking with it" can allow the information to sink in so that it can more effectively reach out and touch places in the heart it might otherwise not have reached.

The Third Chakra: The Solar Plexus Chakra, Manipura

(Yellow/Golden Yellow)

The solar plexus chakra and the one directly below it, the navel chakra, have a great deal in common. Both have to do with the innate power of the individual. The solar plexus chakra residing, as it does, just below the heart chakra, deals with the effect of the emotions on individual power. It is common—and easy—for energy to be blocked in this very active area where all sorts of digestion-related processing goes on.

The physical heart and the lungs are organs of the body that enable us to feel and to express emotions. A person who cannot breathe deeply is physically unable to experience the fullness of emotions. The thoracic diaphragm (at the level of the solar plexus), becomes less flexible from disuse and ends up being a holding place for suppressed emotions. Much of this unintegrated energy is held in the solar plexus chakra, which lies just under the rib cage and includes the stomach, an organ that frequently suffers deep distress from unintegrated emotional upset. Physical indigestion is often an indication of psychological or psychospiritual indigestion.

This type of indigestion, too, manifests in the solar plexus chakra.

The solar plexus chakra is an area that can be highly charged with "stuck" emotions. It is also an area where energy blockage can encircle the body, often causing a very noticeable energetic—and sometimes even physical— "armoring." If the blockage feels severe to you energetically or if the person is experiencing physical pain in the area, you may want to place your left hand back to back with your right hand, the right hand resting palm down over the solar plexus area and the left (palm up), pointing skyward. Call upon your Divine Consciousness, or your angelic team, or some source beyond yourself, and ask for an additional infusion of light. This can be done either aloud or to yourself according to what feels comfortable both to you and your client. The tightness will lessen as the trapped emotions integrate into the body. If there is no change using this position, move the left hand to slide it under the client's back, palm up, radiating into the body from front and back with both hands.

Regarding speaking to other entities during the treatment: there's no problem with this but if it is something that happens for you most times that you work, it's best to advise your client ahead of time that you do so, lest the client thinks that they are the one being addressed. I tend, when energy is flowing fast and hard, to speak in tongues. When it first began to happen, I was taken aback and quite embarrassed by it but I had the good sense to know that by holding back its expression I would also be limiting the energy my client was receiving and so I simply began explaining prior to treatment that it might happen. I never had anyone object ... and once had someone talk back!

Most of what we have called "negative" energy in the past would be better termed misqualified energy, meaning that it feels bad to us. It feels bad because it contains information that we have been unable to integrate and make useful.

We have all chosen to enter into very particular lives for very particular reasons, so there is no reason why we should want to, or need to, dispose of the information that we came here to get. But some of our lessons may occur before we are able to benefit from the information we receive. In such a situation, the information will lie more or less dormant in the body until it is activated. Dormant and unintegrated information can act like a blockage, a place through which the energy cannot flow. Activated, unintegrated information can manifest as pain, disease, or breakdown. The task of Divine Energy is to integrate the stored information, thus allowing the cellular consciousness of the body to shift and change, raising its vibrational level. This is not to say that unneeded, negative energies never exist within a body, for they can and often, when they do, the solar plexus is a place where they are found. The older the blockage, the more excess energy there may be around it.

Should you encounter an excess of energy that seems to have a bad feel to it and which the body seems to reject, then you may draw it off in whatever way suits you or seems appropriate to the situation. This might be a brushing motion, a plucking-out motion, a scooping motion, or any of a variety of movements. The important thing is what happens to this energy once you release it from the body. Try to identify, if you can, which of the elements supplies or feeds the negative energy, and using your intention, return the energy to its source, having neutralized it in the violet transmuting flame.

The violet transmuting flame, or fire, is a field of energy surrounding the body that is activated by consciousness, which is to say that thinking about it makes it work. The violet transmuting flame transmutes misqualified energy into neutral, useful energy.

Angry energy or excess sexual energy comes from fire. Grief, misery, depression, and other "down" energies usually come from water. Excessive thinking comes from air. (Have you ever noticed how difficult it is to quiet your mind on a really windy day?) Disturbances in the make-up of the physical body (tumors, for instance) come from earth energy. Where the energies of disturbances come from is usually fairly obvious. Sometimes, though, the stuck energy is no more than a sort of "glue" holding a blockage in place. In that case, just return the energy to the violet transmuting flame for recycling.

Our bodies draw their energy from the elements. While the elements are a boundless source, they too must draw energy from somewhere. Energy, as you probably already know, is never created or destroyed. It simply is. It seems only right and respectful that, since these elements are helping us, we help them as we can. And one of the things we can do is return their recycled and purified energy to them so they will continue to be productive. Since the energy of the elements is always untainted before it becomes polarized in material form, we ask, as we remove it, that it be neutralized in the violet transmuting flame that purifies all things, so that we can return the energies to their source much as they were given to us. Our intention and our request are all that are needed to accomplish this task.

Sometimes you may find at a later treatment that some of the energy you released from your client seems to have returned. Stuck energies or blockages gather more and more energy around themselves, layer by layer, as time goes on. When you first see the person you will be able to integrate only as much of the energy as they are willing or able to deal with at that time.

It may seem odd, but often a person is simply used to being the way they are and too much change would cause more personal disturbance than they are prepared to handle. Instead, they will integrate bit by bit, layer by layer, over time. It is not the *same* energy you have found but other layers of energy, once hidden, that have now been allowed to surface.

The Navel Chakra and the Hara

(Yellow/Gold)

These two powerful chakras are also not a part of the numbered system of central chakras but they are vitally important.

The navel chakra sits right where you might imagine it would, in the umbilicus. And three body inches (measured by the individual's three fingers) below the navel chakra is the hara. The hara is the central gathering place for energy in the body. It is the area where you focus concentration when you need to access your greatest strength. Breathing into the hara brings a sense of power into the physical body so profound that it generates a feeling of security that is unshakable. This combination of physical strength and security is reflected in the navel chakra.

The navel chakra is the area of innate physical power and peace, our first connection to life. In a satisfied state, the navel chakra feels warm, soft, and relatively calm. If it does not feel this way, bridging is an effective way to restore it to that condition. Bridging consists of placing your forearms across the body on either side of the area that you wish to work with. (In the case of the navel chakra you might lay one arm across the belly and the other across the diaphragm.) Imagine or visualize a broad blanket of gentle energy flowing between your arms, and you will create the desired effect! Check the chakra area itself occasionally with your left hand to see if balance has been restored. Always remember to check the balance with the heart chakra. Balance between the feeling center and power is essential.

The Second Chakra: The Sacral Plexus, Svadhistana

(Orange/Emerald Green)

The sacral plexus chakra is known by many other names including the sexual chakra, the relationship chakra, and the creative center. Svadhistana means, loosely translated, *Her Majesty's Favorite Resort*. Svadhistana is the chakra of creative energy and enjoyment, generation and regeneration. Physically, it lies in the territory of the internal sexual organs, that's the "generation" part. Psychospiritually, it lives in the area of the body that responds to physical pleasure, that's the "re-generation" part. While the root chakra generates the primal energy needed to maintain a healthy sex drive, it is the sacral plexus chakra that, by opening to the sheer joy and physical pleasure of sexual activities, ensures the continuation of the species.

The sacral plexus is also where the creative drive is centered. A person who has stifled or ignored her creative drive and is blocked in this area is also apt to be limited in her enjoyment of other pleasures of life. Creativity and the ability to enjoy are closely linked. A blocked sacral plexus chakra will often feel literally cold or empty. If overactive, the area may feel as though it is on fire, and the energy may need to be redistributed by drawing it down the legs and out the feet or brushing it away from the area into the violet transmuting fire. Always check the balance between the heart chakra and the sacral plexus chakra. The energy levels should feel about equal. If they do not, simply leave your hands in place, one over each chakra, and allow balance to occur. Then, leaving one hand on the sacral plexus chakra, move the hand that was on the heart chakra to the crown and the third eye chakras to see how the balance feels between those areas. Very often, if the heart and the sacral plexus chakras are out of balance it is because of an overactive mental function, so it is important to check the head for that balance as well. Once again, if there is any discrepancy between the two, simply hold in place and allow balance to occur. Then, recheck the heart/sacral plexus balance again before proceeding.

A Word about Kundalini

Kundalini is the name given to the life force energy that is said to be coiled at the base of the spine, in a serpent-like fashion. It is generally regarded among those who study and work with the energy of the human body to be a sort of source-point, anchoring us to the Divine Fire/Life Force that we carry. There are various types of yogic practices that are said to be able to open one up to a vibrant flow of kundalini; such an endeavor is a very personal thing and has no place on a healing table ... unless it happened as a totally spontaneous event for the person involved, which seems rather unlikely. The "breakthrough" of the kundalini energy is not something to be engineered by an outside force; it is something that must originate within a person and can be, should a person not be prepared for such a breakthrough, both physically and mentally devastating. It can also be quite shocking even when a person has been well prepared.

If you have a client that is interested in exploring kundalini and you are not an expert, trained in that area, recommend that they find one.

The First Chakra: The Root Chakra, the Muladhara

(Red/Sapphire Blue)

The root chakra is the source of our basic, primal physical energy. In cases of serious, debilitating illness the root chakra is a reliable determiner of long-term prognosis for healing. A strong energy emanating from the root chakra tells you that the person is a survivor, a fighter. Weak energy indicates a seriously compromised constitution, or someone who has given up hope. This weakness often manifests as depression. In most healthy people the root chakra tends to be as stable in its functioning as the crown chakra, which is almost always open to its connection with Spirit. The root chakra's connection, however, is to the body and to the energy of the earth on which we live.

I would be curious to see how the root chakra would feel on someone who was on the moon just to see how it feels when an earth body is taken to another grounding source! Rumor has it that the first astronauts returned to earth in such sad shape the next group sent out were packing quartz crystals, which are strongly, naturally, programmed with earth energy.

Quartz is famous for being able to hold a charge. The experiment is said to have worked exactly as they hoped it would, grounding and centering the astronauts despite their remote location.

If a person's root chakra feels weakened and you need to flow energy into it, it is most usual to rest your hands along the lines where the tops of the thighs meet the torso on the side of the body and to direct the energy in from there. Polite journaling to the contrary, the actual location of the root chakra is on the pelvic floor just in front of the anus. In most civilized societies, however, it would not be considered either polite or professionally ethical to lay your hands directly on this area. If, however, you are engaged in an intimate relationship with someone needing treatment in that area, you may always ask them how they would feel about your placing your hands directly on the root chakra. Simply aiming the energy toward the area is every bit as effective as on-the-spot treatment, so never feel that the person is getting less than they deserve. Personal comfort levels and ethics are a far greater consideration.

As I mentioned before, there are two reasons why a person's root chakra may feel compromised. In the first instance, that of actual physical weakness, the best thing to do is to flow energy into the chakra. In the second instance, however, that of the person's having given up the will to live, or being depressed, the root chakra will most likely not be the focal point of treatment. More likely the heart chakra, the brain, or both, will need to be treated. Those energies will then need to be balanced with the root chakra. Since the higher chakras are usually treated first, you may well have discovered the source of the disturbance on the way down the body, and the weakness of the root chakra will simply be validating your findings.

Physical weakness stemming from a compromised root chakra may also cause depression, but it is usually the other way around. If your client is a victim of clinical depression, you are unlikely to see improvement in his state of mind from one treatment to the next. Tactfully inform your client of your concern and suggest the possibility of professional psychological assistance.

Chronic fatigue syndrome (CFS) may or may not manifest in the root chakra area depending upon its reason for being with your client in the first place. If you should treat a CFS patient whose condition does show up in the root chakra area, be sure to try the virus treatment with her, and try it on a number of successive occasions, for all the reasons explained under the virus heading earlier in the text. Chronic fatigue syndrome can be a manifest symptom of one or more low-grade viruses present in the body, for where one virus is present, others are usually present also, having taken advantage of a weakened body. Chronic fatigue syndrome can also be, however, a manifest symptom of deep emotional distress that you may or may not be able to address, depending on the person and the circumstances. If you suspect that there is deeply hidden emotion at work, make sure that you express your concerns to the client so that she can work on that with you or obtain other professional help if she so desires.

Be sure to find out, if a client tells you that she has chronic fatigue syndrome, if that determination has been the diagnosis of a physician. Many people do not understand the seriousness of chronic fatigue and feel that they can diagnose themselves. It often turns out that people like this are simply overworked and angry. As in cases of the clinically depressed, if you see no improvement at all (even a change in attitude would be an improvement) after a couple of sessions, it is appropriate to suggest that they seek another sort of professional assistance.

If the root chakra is weak in a seriously ill person because the will to live has left, you will want to discuss this state of body/mind with the person whom you are treating. Some terminally ill people are receiving treatment only because their families want them to continue living. You will need to find out how the person you are working with actually feels about his situation. If the person is comatose and has no say in the matter of his treatment, you can still find out how he feels. You can find out from the root chakra and the heart chakra. You will find that the root chakra feels "weak" or "empty" if your client is approaching transition (death). The emotion you sense in the heart chakra can tell you a great deal about his state of mind, even if he is not conscious. If the heart chakra also feels empty, there is every chance that this person is already in the process of leaving.

Personally, I would not treat a person whose heart says that his body wants to die in the same way that would treat a person whose body expressed the energy of desiring to live. I would be happy to treat a dying person who wants to die in a way that would facilitate his transition, heal his soul, give him courage, or whatever else he may need to make his transition, but I would not attempt to bring him "back to life" no matter what his family might want. I would, of course, discuss this with the family, knowing full well that it would be quite likely that my services would no longer be desired by them.

If the root chakra feels strong, that's another story, because then you know that the body is fighting to live. Attempting to bring a person with an empty heart chakra but a strong root chakra "back to life" will usually yield rapid results, but further healing at the emotional level will probably be called for following convalescence.

Be sure to be open with the appropriate parties about the information you receive. A fully functioning patient deserves to have his or her privacy respected. But a patient who is comatose deserves your utmost honesty when reporting to the person who has brought you onto the case. The fact that you have felt a comatose person's desire to leave may not be well received by families unwilling to let go of a loved one, but integrity is critical in this type of delicate situation. Your commitment in such a situation is twofold. You owe both the patient and the concerned person who brought you in an honest report of his or her condition ... even if it means that your services will "no longer be required." Integrity must always be honored as it is your reflection of who you are and what you do.

The Knee Chakras

(Rainbow)

While the knees are frequently ignored in many chakra texts, which tend to concentrate on everything from the groin up for some strange reason, the knees are very important and telling areas on the human body. The knees are energetically linked to the kidneys and, as such, are good barometers for the extent to which the emotion of fear is operating in the body. A person with weak or sore knees is a person who may be dealing with fear on some level, and that level may go back as far as early childhood or even earlier.

Begin your work here by gently resting a hand on each patella (knee cap). If you feel jerky movements beneath your hands, or something that feels like popcorn popping, then you know for sure that the knees need work.

Cradle one knee gently between your hands—placed on the inside and the outside of the leg—and allow energy to flow from one hand to the other through and around the area behind the patella. Do this until the sensation of physical disturbance subsides. Then slide one hand beneath that knee and rest the other on top and again flow the energy between your hands until the area feels peaceful. Then attend to the other knee.

If the knees are quite bad, having suffered years of mistreatment (as is often the case), work until you are confident that the disturbance has at least been lessened. Severely damaged knees can heal remarkably well but often need many short repeat visits to do the job. A body in which fear has been ingrained may need to feel very secure before it lets go of the emotion completely. Or there may be so much fear present or so much emotional damage done that the body needs to integrate information in small doses to allow the healing to unfold.

Because fear so affects a person's relationship with the rest of the world, the knees are also a good place to discover how a person relates to others. This knowledge is especially important for people whose lives involve dealing with the public.

The Foot Chakras

(Black/Maroon/Brown)

Feet are incredibly important energetically! Feet are our connection with our mother planet. Think of all the popular phrases we have that relate us to our earth: "got his feet on the ground," "a real down-to-earth person," "grounded," "salt of the earth." It's no coincidence that every language has its own version of phrases like these. If the chakras of your feet are not wide open to the energy of the earth then you are missing a good deal of energetic fuel, and this is exactly what happens to a person who spends most of his time living in his head. Too much cerebration, not enough celebration!

The more technological our society has become the farther we have gotten from our roots. (There's another one of those phrases!) In cities, there's very little unadulterated earth on which to set your feet, and it takes well-developed foot chakras to connect to the earth through rubber-soled shoes! Oh yes, it *can* be done and is done every day, but only by the very grounded and the very conscious.

Hold your client's feet, both at once, resting your hands on ankles at the outside of the leg, then cradling the bottoms of the feet, then one foot at a time holding the foot both top and bottom between both hands, then your right hand on the top of their left foot and your left on their right. (In a person who is dying, cross your arms, putting your left hand on their left foot, your right hand on their right foot. This seems to allow for a little loosening from the natural grounding.)

Play around with feeling the energy balancing between the feet. As you hold the feet be very conscious of feeling your own groundedness. Let their body learn from yours. When things start feeling good, grab each foot and tug the leg gently. If the body responds by jumping in a slightly startled fashion, then you've got more work to do. Try holding one hand on one foot while moving your other hand to the knee of that same leg. Then move that hand from the knee to the thigh/torso area, still holding the foot with the other hand. When you do this you are, in effect, energetically connecting the leg to the torso. Repeat on the other leg in a similar fashion then go back to the feet again and hold them for a while before testing out your results with another gentle tug.

In extreme cases, for instance when treating someone who has attention deficit disorder, you may spend quite a bit of time on the feet. Don't give up! It can be done, and do not move on from there; continue until it is. Just remember to be aware of your *own* grounding.

Some attunements open the chakras of the feet of the initiate to allow the energies of the earth to flow more freely through the body. This is done to increase the initiates grounding energy, allowing him to ground others more efficiently. Just as a tree can only extend its branches as far out as its roots go, we can only draw in from Spirit to the extent that we can ground our bodies.

Closing a Healing Session

When working with a client you become intimately involved with her energetic fields. Before ending a treatment be very conscious to disconnect from her, returning responsibility for her healing to her. (I actually do this aloud, making it sound as if I am giving the person a gift.) Then, consciously, pull out of, and detach from, her energy field. I have created for myself a symbol that I use to "disconnect" myself from my client when a session is complete; you may wish to do something similar if it feels appropriate for you.

Since receiving a healing treatment is very relaxing, you may find that the person on whom you are working has fallen sound asleep! When the treatment is over, speak softly, informing her that the work is completed. Tell her that she can open her eyes whenever she is ready, that she should take her time returning to full and functional consciousness. If more than a couple of minutes should pass by with no response, speak again. This time you may want to gently jiggle one of her feet.

When you sense that she is about to get up, you can instruct her on the proper way to rise from the table: tell her to roll to her right side, swing her legs down off the table and push up with her arms. This is easy on the heart and, therefore, puts less stress on the body.

Once she is seated on the table ask her how she feels. Sometimes a person may feel dizzy or just a little "out of it" when first getting up from the table after energy work. If this is the case, assure her that you will assist in returning her to full consciousness, ask her to remain seated and walk around the table, behind her. Place one hand on either side of her spine and, using light to medium pressure on her back, draw the energy down the spine to the table. Do this three times. (You cannot do this work in the auric field; you need to have physical contact with the body. If you have been working only in the auric field, remember to warn the person that you are actually going to touch their back.) When you have finished, walk around to her front to ask how she is feeling. Meet her eyes so that you can read subtleties that she may not be communicating to you.

If the answer you receive is in any way tentative, or if the look in her eyes tells you that she is still in somewhat of a healing trance, have her remain seated and hold her feet, one at a time, placing one of your hands beneath the foot and using your other hand to hold the two hollow spots just beneath the anklebones on either side. Press gently on these two areas; ideally the pressure is barely noticeable.

This should do it! But if it doesn't, just start over at the spine and, should you get all the way back to the feet again, rub the soles of her feet vigorously. Be sure to rinse your hands, or in some other way cleanse and clear yourself before returning to another activity.

Energy Healing Following a Physical Healing

People who have endured profound, chronic, long-term illnesses have had very serious lessons to learn. If such a person receives energetic healing later in life, after physical healing from the disease process has already taken place, he may very well experience the return of sensations that he associates with the former illness. This is nothing to be afraid of! It is something to be grateful for as the return of these sensations will allow him to review his former disease in a new, enlightened way. It emphatically does not mean that the disease is coming back! It is only the body's way of asking to be heard this time as it may not have been heard prior to the physical healing.

You certainly would not want to alarm someone by saying that his old symptoms may come back again once he has received a treatment, for that is not what happens. What happens, when it happens (which is rare), is that phantom symptoms appear. Phantom symptoms are like dream symptoms; they may feel real but all they are, are reminders of information that has remained unintegrated by the body consciousness, information that must be integrated for deep healing to occur. If you suspect that such a thing may happen to someone on whom you have worked, merely leave him with the reminder to call you if he has any questions about the changes his body may go through in the next few days. If he calls with concerns, saying that he is "feeling the same as when ..." or if he is actually experiencing phantom sensations, you now know how to handle it. Be upbeat and positive always! Your attitude is contagious ... and important to your client's state of mind. He will hear in your tone of voice that what he is experiencing is a validation of his continued healing and that will most likely please him.

Medical science has found many ways to fix diseases, but bodies in which diseases are only *fixed* can "break" again. Disease may well return if the person has not healed from whatever emotional or psychological trauma may have caused the disturbance/dis-ease in the first place. The return of phantom symptoms can allow a person to consciously explore what it is that the body has been trying to tell them, so that they can heal in a more complete way, body, mind, and soul.

Cleansing the Treatment Area

Just as you cleanse yourself after performing healing work on someone, you need to cleanse—or clear—the space in which you have been working. When I first began my private practice, I used to keep a lit candle burning in the room, figuring that it would burn off any untoward energies. It may have, but, as I discovered when I prepared to repaint the room, it had also coated all four walls with soot ... that couldn't be good! It felt to me as if the negative energies had been clinging to the walls, as if this burning desire I had to repaint had been subconsciously fueled by a build-up of, well, who knows what.

I did some research and uncovered information on using vibration to clear space. It seems that a very high-pitched tone will penetrate anything, going right through it, and carrying with as it goes, whatever has to get out of its way to be able to so cleanly resonate. I purchased a small but high-quality aluminum chime that could be struck with a small mallet and produced a high E that was not quite ear-splitting. That did the job nicely. Interestingly, I never again experienced that burning desire to repaint!

Ultimately I trained my voice to do the job and ended up using my voice to clear and to balance people as well, directing it at each chakra individually. It's a very doable thing.

A Brief Introduction to Sleep Magic

I have mentioned in this book that the use of the Sleep Magic technique can assist you in becoming the best person you can be, allowing you to become the best healer you can be. Sleep Magic allows you to clear old emotional wounds to your cellular programming, strengthens the relationship that you have with your body and its wisdom, and can increase your creativity exponentially.

You can also teach your clients the technique. By now I have heard from many therapists who are doing this. Teaching your clients to help themselves is empowering for them and displays to them your genuine concern for them as people.

Ozark Mountain Publishing has published *Sleep Magic: Surrender to Success* which is a detailed manual on the many ways that Sleep Magic can be used but, in short, what Sleep Magic is, is surrendering your will to the will of your body. It is you, turning over your concerns about life, to the wisdom of your body and allowing it to help you either accept what you cannot change with grace and comfort or to change what can be changed.

In a nutshell, prior to going to sleep, at any time during the day, you set aside a minute in which you (a) thank your body for everything it does for you, (b) present it with your concern, (c) let it know that it has your permission to shift whatever needs shifting in order to allow you to become more comfortable, and finally, (d) thanking your body for listening and for working with you to become the best you can be.

May you and your body prosper and thrive!

About the Author

Victoria Pendragon was born and raised in the vicinity of Philadelphia, Pennsylvania. She is the oldest of eleven. Her life has been defined, as are most of ours perhaps, by conditions that would seem to have been beyond her control. Eighteen years of various sorts of abuse and two diseases that should have killed her rank among the most outstanding of those.

Victoria Pendragon's study of metaphysics began in early childhood as an attempt to validate the lessons she'd been learning from the earth and the trees whenever she left her body. She has been working in the field of spirituality since 1995. A student of the I Ching since 1966, she has been, since 2000, a passionate student of Human Design as well.

Victoria began training in art when still a child, eventually acquiring a BFA from The Philadelphia College of Art. Her work hangs in numerous corporate and personal collections, among them The Children's Hospital of the University of Pennsylvania, Moss Rehab and Bryn Mawr Hospital Rehab.

Victoria Pendragon has two children by her first marriage, a son and a daughter, both of whom amaze her. She is currently married to her third husband, a man whose kind soul has created for her an atmosphere of clarity and creativity in which she dances, writes, creates art and helps when asked.

Books by Victoria Pendragon

Feng Shui From the Inside, Out
Published by: Ozark Mountain Publishing

Sleep Magic
Published by: Ozark Mountain Publishing

The Grail: A Beginners Guide to Spiritual Realization, Self-Actualization & Metaphysics
On 8 CDs, Self-Published

My Three Years as A Tree
Self-Published

The Little Chakra Book
Self-Published

OZARK
MOUNTAIN
PUBLISHING

For more information about any of the above titles, soon to be released titles, or other items in our catalog, write, phone or visit our website:
Ozark Mountain Publishing, LLC
PO Box 754, Huntsville, AR 72740
479-738-2348/800-935-0045
www.ozarkmt.com

If you liked this book, you might also like:

My Teachers Wear Fur Coats
by Susan Mack & Natalia Krawetz

Why Healing Happens
by O.T. Bonnett

Raising Our Vibrations
by Sherri Cortland

Feng Shui From the Inside, Out
by Victoria Pendragon

Soul Choices: Six Paths to Find Your Life Purpose
by Kathryn Andries

Let's Get Natural with Herbs
by Debra Rayburn

What Happens After Medical School
by O.T. Bonnett

For more information about any of the above titles, soon to be released titles,
or other items in our catalog, write, phone or visit our website:

Ozark Mountain Publishing, LLC
PO Box 754, Huntsville, AR 72740
479-738-2348
www.ozarkmt.com

Other Books By Ozark Mountain Publishing, LLC

Dolores Cannon
A Soul Remembers Hiroshima
Between Death and Life
Conversations with Nostradamus,
    Volume I, II, III
The Convoluted Universe -Book One,
    Two, Three, Four, Five
The Custodians
Five Lives Remembered
Jesus and the Essenes
Keepers of the Garden
Legacy from the Stars
The Legend of Starcrash
The Search for Hidden Sacred Knowledge
They Walked with Jesus
The Three Waves of Volunteers and the
    New Earth
Aron Abrahamsen
Holiday in Heaven
Out of the Archives – Earth Changes
Justine Alessi & M. E. McMillan
Rebirth of the Oracle
Kathryn/Patrick Andries
Naked In Public
Kathryn Andries
The Big Desire
Dream Doctor
Soul Choices: Six Paths to Find Your Life
    Purpose
Soul Choices: Six Paths to Fulfilling
    Relationships
Tom Arbino
You Were Destined to be Together
Rev. Keith Bender
The Despiritualized Church
O.T. Bonnett, M.D./Greg Satre
Reincarnation: The View from Eternity
What I Learned After Medical School
Why Healing Happens
Julia Cannon
Soul Speak – The Language of Your Body
Ronald Chapman
Seeing True
Albert Cheung
The Emperor's Stargate
Jack Churchward
Lifting the Veil on the Lost Continent of Mu
The Stone Tablets of Mu
Sherri Cortland
Guide Group Fridays
Raising Our Vibrations for the New Age
Spiritual Tool Box
Windows of Opportunity
Cinnamon Crow
Chakra Zodiac Healing Oracle
Teen Oracle
Michael Dennis
Morning Coffee with God

God's Many Mansions
Claire Doyle Beland
Luck Doesn't Happen by Chance
Jodi Felice
The Enchanted Garden
Max Flindt/Otto Binder
Mankind: Children of the Stars
Arun & Sunanda Gandhi
The Forgotten Woman
Maiya & Geoff Gray-Cobb
Angels -The Guardians of Your Destiny
Seeds of the Soul
Julia Hanson
Awakening To Your Creation
Donald L. Hicks
The Divinity Factor
Anita Holmes
Twidders
Antoinette Lee Howard
Journey Through Fear
Vara Humphreys
The Science of Knowledge
Victoria Hunt
Kiss the Wind
James H. Kent
Past Life Memories As A Confederate
    Soldier
Mandeep Khera
Why?
Dorothy Leon
Is Jehovah An E.T
Mary Letorney
Discover The Universe Within You
Sture Lönnerstrand
I Have Lived Before
Irene Lucas
Thirty Miracles in Thirty Days
Susan Mack & Natalia Krawetz
My Teachers Wear Fur Coats
Patrick McNamara
Beauty and the Priest
Maureen McGill
Baby It's You
Maureen McGill & Nola Davis
Live From the Other Side
Henry Michaelson
And Jesus Said – A Conversation
Dennis Milner
Kosmos
Guy Needler
Avoiding Karma
Beyond the Source – Book 1, Book 2
The History of God
The Origin Speaks
James Nussbaumer
The Master of Everything
Sherry O'Brian
Peaks and Valleys

Other Books By Ozark Mountain Publishing, LLC

Riet Okken
The Liberating Power of Emotions
John Panella
The Gnostic Papers
Victor Parachin
Sit a Bit
Nikki Pattillo
A Spiritual Evolution
Children of the Stars
Rev. Grant H. Pealer
A Funny Thing Happened on the
    Way to Heaven
Worlds Beyond Death
Karen Peebles
The Other Side of Suicide
Victoria Pendragon
Feng Shui from the Inside, Out
Sleep Magic
Michael Perlin
Fantastic Adventures in Metaphysics
Walter Pullen
Evolution of the Spirit
Christine Ramos, RN
A Journey Into Being
Debra Rayburn
Let's Get Natural With Herbs
Charmian Redwood
A New Earth Rising
Coming Home to Lemuria
David Rivinus
Always Dreaming
Briceida Ryan
The Ultimate Dictionary of Dream
    Language
M. Don Schorn
Elder Gods of Antiquity
Legacy of the Elder Gods

Gardens of the Elder Gods
Reincarnation...Stepping Stones of Life
Garnet Schulhauser
Dancing Forever with Spirit
Dancing on a Stamp
Annie Stillwater Gray
Education of a Guardian Angel
The Dawn Book
Blair Styra
Don't Change the Channel
Natalie Sudman
Application of Impossible Things
L.R. Sumpter
We Are the Creators
Dee Wallace/Jarrad Hewett
The Big E
Dee Wallace
Conscious Creation
James Wawro
Ask Your Inner Voice
Janie Wells
Payment for Passage
Dennis Wheatley/ Maria Wheatley
The Essential Dowsing Guide
Jacquelyn Wiersma
The Zodiac Recipe
Sherry Wilde
The Forgotten Promise
Stuart Wilson & Joanna Prentis
Atlantis and the New Consciousness
Beyond Limitations
The Essenes -Children of the Light
The Magdalene Version
Power of the Magdalene
Robert Winterhalter
The Healing Christ

For more information about any of the above titles, soon to be released titles,
or other items in our catalog, write, phone or visit our website:
PO Box 754, Huntsville, AR 72740
479-738-2348/800-935-0045
www.ozarkmt.com